Published by Aperitifs Publishing Company
Santa Rosa, California 95404
707-523-1611
johncburton@msn.com

Mike Capitani
Email: zepsandwings@yahoo.com

ISBN: 979-8-218-36194-5
Library of Congress Number: 2024901480

Copyright January 2024
Compiled by John C. Burton

Printed in the United States of America

Every attempt has been made to provide accurate information on the following subjects.

FORWARD

I was not particularly interested in Santa Rosa or Sonoma County history when I was growing up in Santa Rosa. My interest began after high school, when I went looking for information about my great-grandfather Peter Maroni, the Italian Stone Mason who with others, built several stone buildings in Santa Rosa and Sonoma County.

In the 1980s I found the only photo I have of him on an office wall in the old Traverso deli, which was located in downtown Santa Rosa. Since then, I have spent the last 40 years collecting early Santa Rosa and Sonoma County postcards, photos, artifacts, and collectibles. Many of my collectibles were located outside of the area and I'm happy to have brought those items back to Santa Rosa.

I've been lucky in my life to have known people who have guided me in my quest for Santa Rosa and Sonoma County history. Notably, Gaye LeBaron, Sonoma County's Historian, sharing her knowledge and writings, making history come alive.

John Schubert, my friend, along with Harry & Lily Lapham and Ann Connor, who I served with in the past as a member of the Sonoma County Historical Society.

John Rovetti, an "old time" Santa Rosan, who has shared his memories and collection of Santa Rosa and Sonoma County's history as well as his collection of the Hoag family.

John Burton and Dennis Kurlander, both who have shared information and personal collections with me.

To the countless others, antique dealers, flea market sellers, those that I've met at estate and garage sales, fellow collectors and acquaintances, thank you all.

I cannot forget to mention the valuable information I've learned from the Santa Rosa Press Democrat and Santa Rosa Republican newspapers. And to the staff at the Sonoma County genealogical and history library annex.

I thank you all, Mike Capitani

IN MEMORY OF JOHN SCHUBERT
I would like to dedicate this my first book to John Schubert, my friend.

John Schubert – Mike Capitani – Sarah Brooks

A SHORT FAMILY HISTORY

My family came to Santa Rosa before the turn of the century. Santa Rosa, before 1900, was a small town that seemed to be waiting for my great-grandfather, Peter Maroni, an Italian Stone Mason.

Peter Maroni and others started building Sonoma County's basalt block buildings: Kenwood's Train Depot, St. Rose Church, Santa Rosa's Carnegie Library, Western Hotel, Railroad Train Depot & Railroad Express Office, the Hop Kiln Dryer in Healdsburg (now a winery), Healdsburg Grammer School, The Nervo Winery in Geyserville (now Trione Winery) and Jack London Wolf House.

II

CONTENTS

Santa Rosa, California

STREET SCENE IN SANTA ROSA

The County Seat of Sonoma County

Santa Rosa has

5 Banks	2 Excellent Hotels	1 Flour Mill	1 Brewery
4 Fruit Canneries	1 Woolen Mill	Fruit Drying Factories	
2 Tanneries	2 Lumber Yards	Street Cars	

Municipal water works, with free water, free rural delivery and is situated in the heart of **Stock Growing, Grain Farming, Hop Raising, Fruit Growing,** of Sonoma County

Excellent Public and Private Schools, Churches and Lodges. Excellent climate year round. Population 10,000. 52 miles from San Francisco; 5 trains daily to and from city. Gas and electric light. Telephones. Plenty of good land for sale cheap. For further information address any of the following:

The Sonoma County Abstract Bureau.
Santa Rosa Bank.
Occidental Hotel Co.
Santa Rosa National Bank.
J. P. Fitts Lumber Co.

Houts, Jewell & Peterson, Real Estate
Eardley & Barnett, Real Estate.
W. D. Reynolds, Real Estate.
F. Berka, Lumber.
Lee Bros. & Co., Draymen.

COURT HOUSE & CITY HALL

Sonoma County Court House pre 1906 Earthquake

Side view of above card

Plaque with Supervisor Names on 1890 Court House Entrance

Steel Structure of Sonoma County Court House

Rebuilding the Court House After 1906 Earthquake

Presenting the Trowel for laying the Court House Cornerstone

Court House illuminated for the N.S.G.W. Celebration

Sonoma County Court House as our generation knew it prior to 1969 Earthquake

Fourth Street view, notice Trolley

2435. - INTERIOR SONOMA COUNTY COURT HOUSE, SANTA ROSA, CALIFORNIA.

Interior of Sonoma County Court House
City Fathers Voted to Remove Building for Urban Renewal

1834 - General View and Court House, Santa Rosa, California.

Corner Fourth Street & Hinton Avenue
No Automobiles in Photo

CITY HALL AND COUNTY JAIL SANTA ROSA CAL.

City Hall & County Jail on Hinton Avenue

ITALIAN STONE MASONS

HEALDSBURG GRAMMAR SCHOOL
CIRCA 1906

Peter Maroni (1860-1919), an Italian stonemason, who along with other stonemasons, built many of the main basalt stone buildings in Sonoma County. Peter Maroni sitting on left side & Augustus Deghi sitting on right side of arch.

Kenwood Train Depot	1887	Main Stone Masons
Saint Rose Church	1900	Peter Maroni
Western Hotel Santa Rosa	1903	Natale Forni
Santa Rosa Library	1903	Angelo Sodini
Santa Rosa Train Depot	1904	Massimo Galeazzi
Hop Kiln Winery Healdsburg	1905	Augustus Deghi
Healdsburg Grammar School	1906	Samuel Sebastiani
La Rose Hotel Santa Rosa	1907	
Nervo Winery Geyserville	1908	
Jack London's Wolf House	1913	
REA Express Office Santa Rosa	1915	

The Swank Quarry, known as Santa Rosa Bank, owned by John Swank, was purchased in 1907 by Peter Maroni, renamed the Titania quarry, and later known as Santa Rosa Bank. The quarry was located in Santa Rosa across from the current Stone House. That stone was used in the La Rose Hotel.

In Kenwood, the Maroni quarry AKA Clute brothers' quarry & later as the Sonoma Farms quarry was operated by Joseph T. Grace.

Approximately in 1914, Maroni worked the Metone quarry three-miles west of Healdsburg for building stones and paving blocks for the United States Army using those blocks in at the Presidio and Fort Baker. The Army contracted for fifteen hundred tons of building stones.

At Stoney Point Quarry, nine-miles south of Sebastapol, Maroni removed enough stone on the northside hill for erection of the new Analy Savings Bank.

Some of the Italian Stonemasons in Santa Rosa and Sonoma County who worked together from time to time were: Peter Maroni, Natale Forni, Angelo Sodini, Massino Galeazzi, Augustus Deghi, and Samuel Sebastiani.

1891-1913, the McDonald quarry was located between 2 to 3 miles east of Santa Rosa. The quarry was 2-miles from the Bava rail-siding. The City of Santa Rosa leased a portion of the quarry for local street stones.

The quarry pits are located between 350 to 400 feet elevation, containing gray andesite rock. Matthews & Company provided a rock crushing plant crushing approximately 30 tons of rock per day. The rock was used for building the Northwestern Pacific Depot, St. Rose Church, and Carnegie Library.

Peter Maroni top left & Augustus Deghi top right of arch with blueprints.

Kenwood Train Depot - 1887

St. Rose Church c. 1909

Western Hotel lower Fourth Street c.1903

Western Hotel Damaged During 1906 Earthquake

**Carnegie Library prior to the 1906 Earthquake
Notice the Small Witch's Hat and Tower Room**

Carnegie Library Restored After 1906 Earthquake

Santa Rosa Northwestern Pacific Train Depot c.1904
Notice original water tower in back of depot
Railroad Square Fourth Street

Hop Kiln Winery Healdsburg 1905

Healdsburg Grammar School c.1906

La Rose Hotel Santa Rosa c.1907
Wilson Street

Nervo Winery Geyserville 1908
Now Trione Winery

Jack London Wolf House Glen Ellen c. 1913
Destroyed By Fire Before Completed

REA Express Office Santa Rosa c.1915
Now A'Roma Roasters

Overall View of Railroad Square
Lower Fourth Street

HORSE & BUGGY DAYS
Pre 1906 Earthquake

1832- Fire Department, Santa Rosa, California.

Santa Rosa Fire Department

Fourth Street Rail Car to McDonald Avenue

Third Street Grand Hotel on the left

Notice "Cow Catcher" on front of trolley

To McDonald neighborhood with trolley service

Republican News Office on Exchange Avenue

Looking at corner Fourth & Main (Mendocino) Streets

Topographical view of looking at corner of Fourth & Main (Mendocino) Streets

California Restaurant & Boraxo Laundry Soap advertisement on left

Trolley tracks running down middle of Fourth Street from A Street

Trolley tracks, bicycles and horse & buggy transportation

Fourth St. Looking West, Santa Rosa, Cal.

Santa Rosa Savings Bank on the left

Court House facing Fourth Street with trolley car in front

Exchange Avenue Hahman Drug Store & Santa Rosa Savings Bank

Busy Street scene on Fourth Street with approaching trolley

Hunt Brothers Fruit Packing Plant Lower Fourth Street across the train tracks

ANTHEAUM – RIDGEWAY HALL
Most major events were held at Ridgway Hall

INVITATION PARTY.

Select Thanksgiving Masquerade.

TO BE GIVEN AT

Ridgway Hall, Santa Rosa, Thursday Evening, November 28th, 1878.

Mr. ___

Yourself and Ladies are Cordially Invited.

GRAND MARCH AT 9:30.   INVITATIONS NOT TRANSFERABLE.

Tickets, admitting Gentleman and Ladies, $2 00.

CAMP ORTON AT ARGYLE PARK – SANTA ROSA
At the end of McDonald Ave, Before
Development of the Surrounding Area
Current Property of Presbyterian Church
(California National Guard Training Exercise)

1ˢᵗ. Inft. Regt. N. G. C. - Santa Rosa, July 20ᵗʰ – 29ᵗʰ, 1889

Dress Parade

Company B Camp – Argyle Park

Day Break Campfire - Camp Orton at Argyle Park

FIRST POSITION OF A SOLDIER.

Camp Orton Initiation

Surgeon's Quarters – Camp Orton at Argyle Park Santa Rosa 1889

1906 EARTHQUAKE
Before & After the 1906 Earthquake

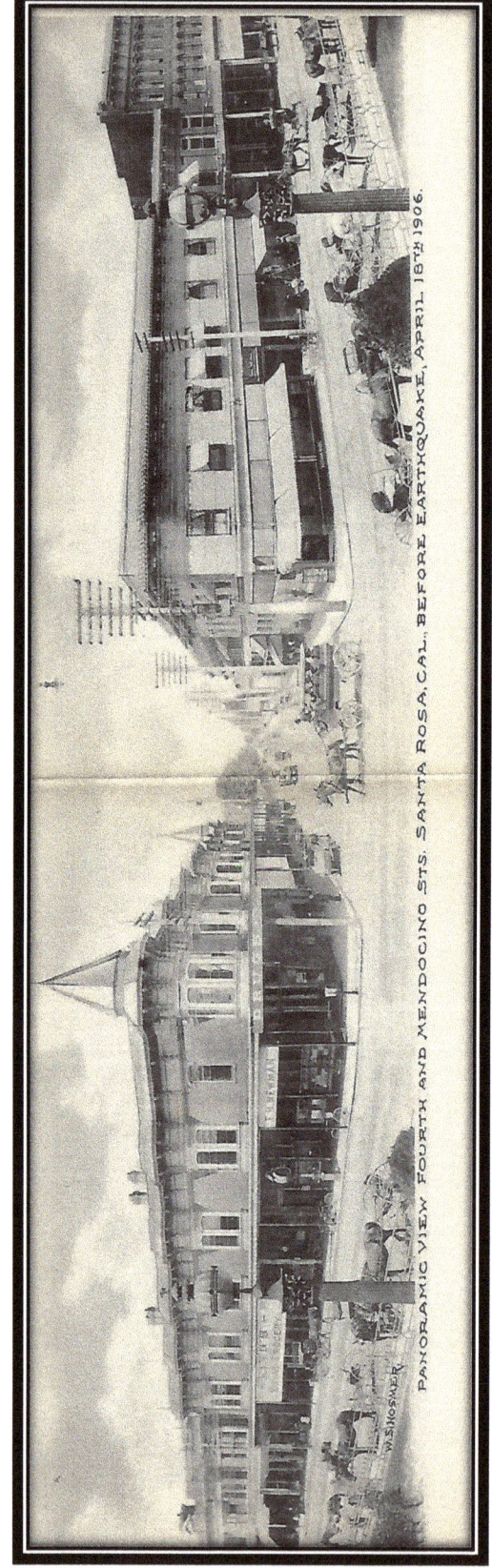

Sonoma County Court House showing collapsed dome

Frontal view of Sonoma County Court House

Western Hotel Lower Fourth Street

Santa Rosa Savings Bank

Santa Rosa Flour Mill

Kegan Brush Building (Keegan misspelt on card)

Grand Hotel across from the Court House

**Stunned, frightened community and personal world totally disrupted
Santa Rosa caught the "whip" of the earthquake**

Fourth street, Santa Rosa, Cal., after the earthquake and fire, April 18, 1906.
Published by the Rieder-Cardinell Co., Los Angeles and Oakland

**Imagine the clean-up by horse & buggy. All manual labor. Believed to be
Luther Burbank standing on left of post card wearing white hat.**

Wrecking Train – Cleanup operation - Where do you start?

Overall view of earthquake damage

All churches in Santa Rosa suffered damage but were left standing

MEDICAL HOSPITALS & SANITARIUMS

Frontal view of Santa Rosa Hospital at 714 Humboldt Street

Interior of Santa Rosa Hospital showing staff

Mary Jesse Hospital 5ᵗʰ Street

Entrance to Mary Jesse Hospital

Bacci Drug Store token located at 401 Mendocino Avenue
Mary Jesse Hospital staff

Mary Jesse Hospital Calendar 1914

No. 1 Johnson's First Aid Kit Capitani collection

Doctor's Indispensable Traveling Kit - Capitani collection

1924 Santa Rosa Phone Book

Sonoma County Hospital on Chanate Road in Santa Rosa which is still standing today

Burke's Sanitarium framed photos
Advertisement piece that was hung in a train depot

Dr. Burke viewing the grounds

Burke's Sanitarium Santa Rosa, Cal   4946

Burkes Sanitarium on Mark West Road Santa Rosa

Annex at Dr. Burkes Sanitarium

GROUP OF TENTS AT DR. BURKE'S SANITARIUM, BURKE, SONOMA CO., CAL

Patients Living Quarters at Dr. Burkes Sanitarium

Jenner Sanitarium in Santa Rosa

Physicians Call List & Record Book listing patient records & medications

Sonoma County Library Collection

HAHMAN'S
ALMOND
CREAM
For Chapped hands and Face
Sunburn or Tan
SOOTHING AND HEALING
25 Cents a Bottle
Hahman's Family Drug Store
Prescriptions a Specialty   215 Exchange Ave.
Press Democrat
May 1898

Sonoma County Library Collection
Hahman Drug Company rebuilt on Exchange Avenue after 1906 Earthquake

Two views of interior of Hahman Drug Store
Sonoma County Library Collection

Sonoma County Library Collection

Hahman Drug Company Coin Purse
Promotional Item

Belden & Upp Prescription Druggist 1908 located at 433 Fourth Street in Occidental Hotel

St. Rose Drug Store, Wm. McK. Stewart proprietor
Northeast corner Fourth & A Streets

St. Rose Drug Store Fourth & A Streets

Earthquake damage next to St. Rose Drug Store

Tomasco's Pharmacy 305 Fourth Street c. 1915

J. W. Warboys, *Druggist and Apothecary*,
511 FOURTH STREET, SANTA ROSA.

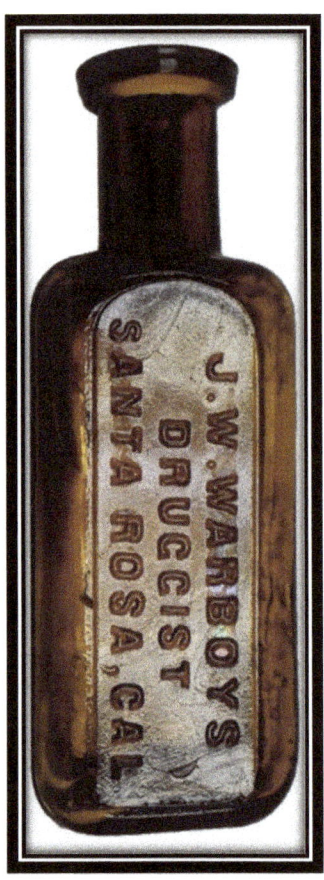

COMPLIMENTS OF
C. D. FRAZEE,
Santa Rosa.

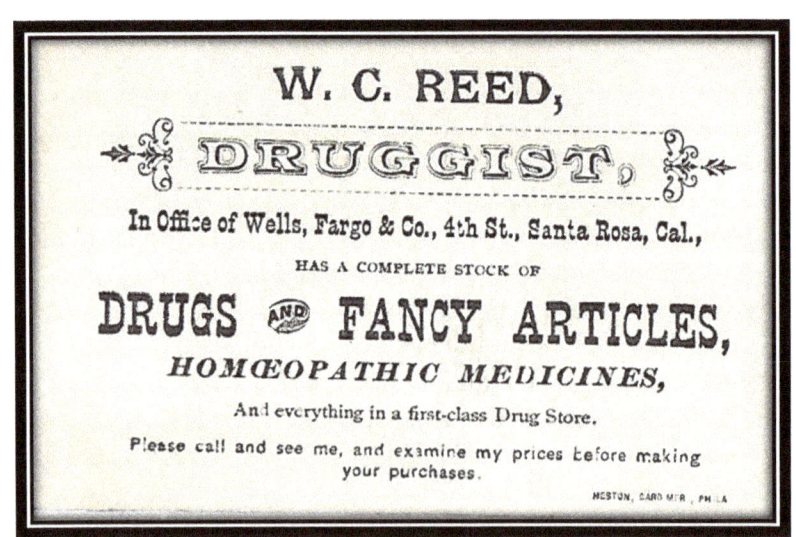

W. C. REED,

DRUGGIST,

In Office of Wells, Fargo & Co., 4th St., Santa Rosa, Cal.,

HAS A COMPLETE STOCK OF

DRUGS AND FANCY ARTICLES,

HOMŒOPATHIC MEDICINES,

And everything in a first-class Drug Store.

Please call and see me, and examine my prices before making
your purchases.

HESTON, CARD MFR., PHILA

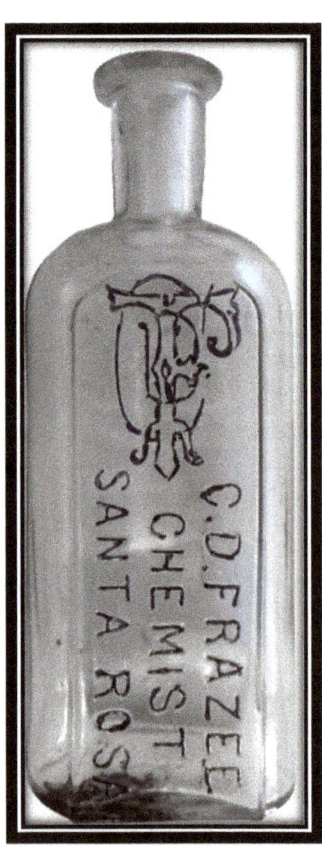

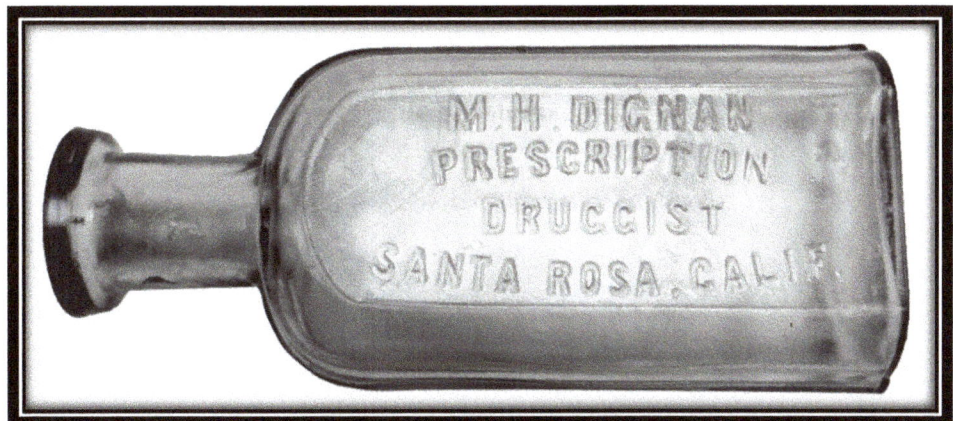

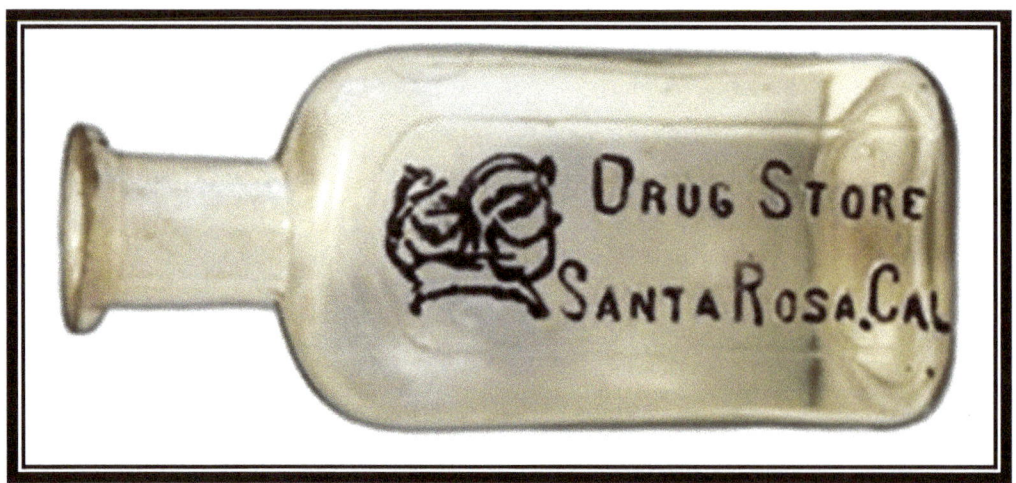

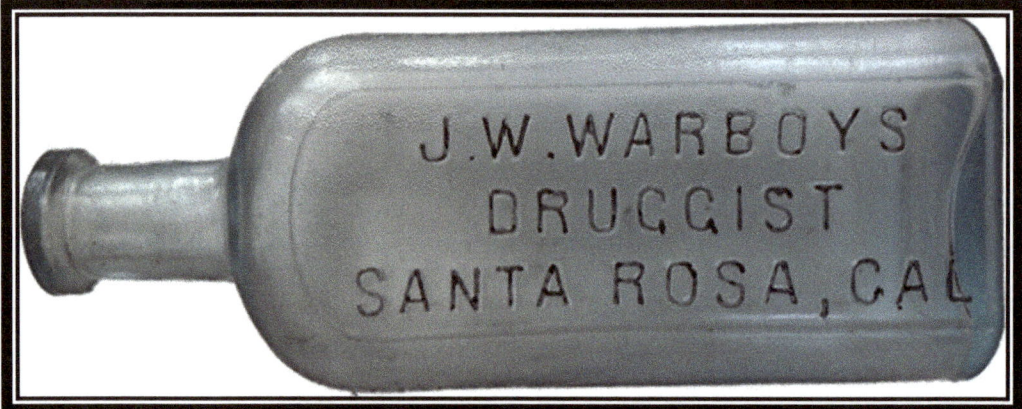

BLUE POISON BOTTLE
Poison bottles were "ribbed" as a warning

Juell's Pharmacy
Nelf Juell Proprietor
215 B Street

Top image three-fold counter advertisement

Countertop cardboard display advertisement

Countertop cardboard display advertisement

Countertop cardboard display advertisement
Part of a three-piece set

Druggist medicine containers

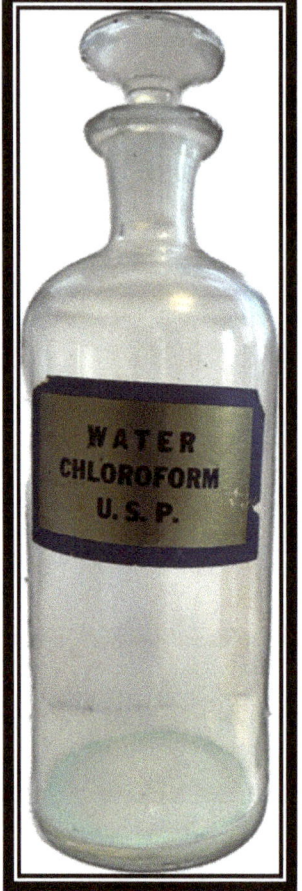
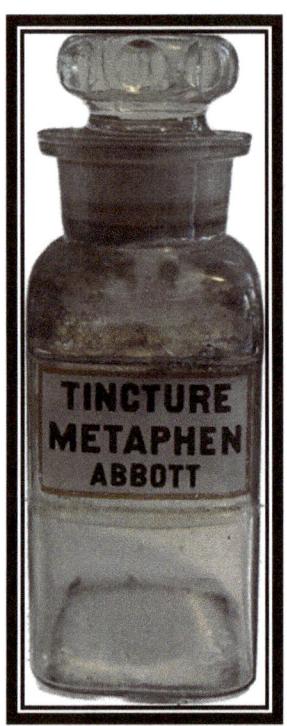

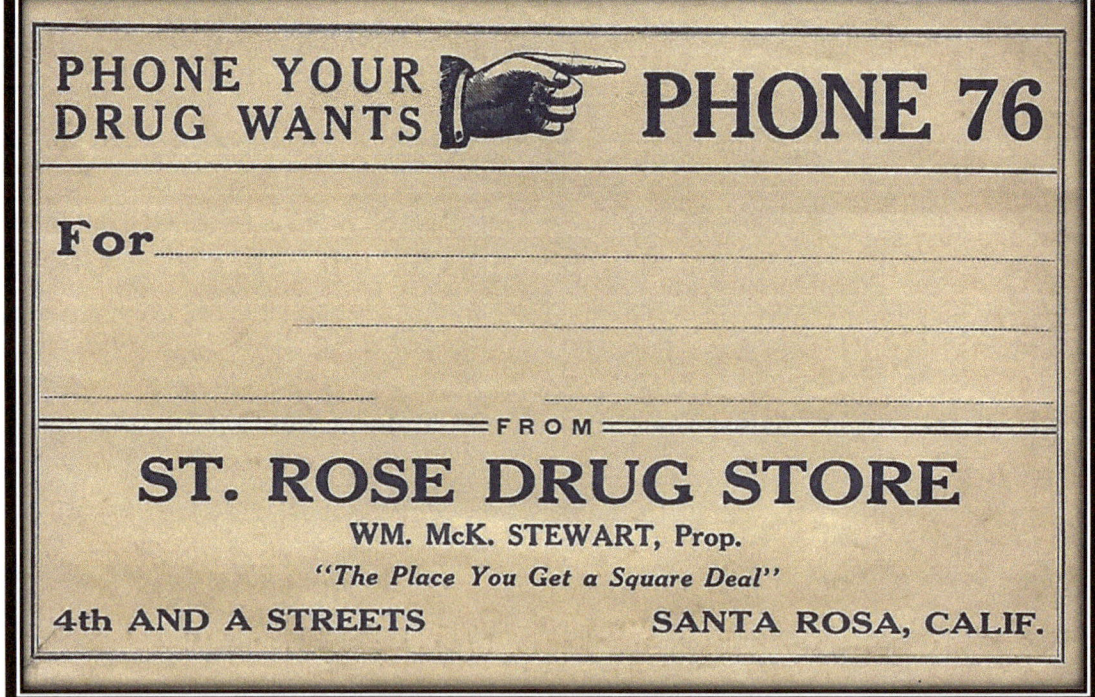

Drug store prescriptions & colorful bandage tins

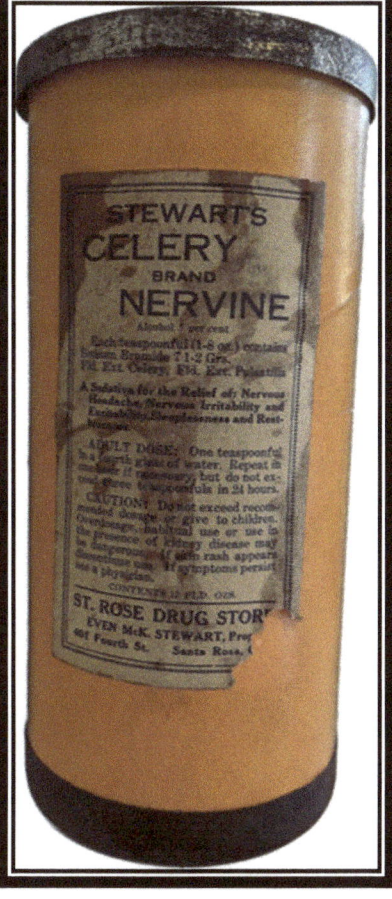

STEWART'S
CELERY
BRAND
NERVINE

ST. ROSE DRUG STORE
EVEN McK. STEWART, Prop.
Fourth St. Santa Rosa, Calif.

PUMICE, N. F.

AN ABRASIVE

DISTRIBUTED BY
MEDICO DRUG CO., Inc.
625 SEBASTOPOL ROAD
SANTA ROSA, CALIF.

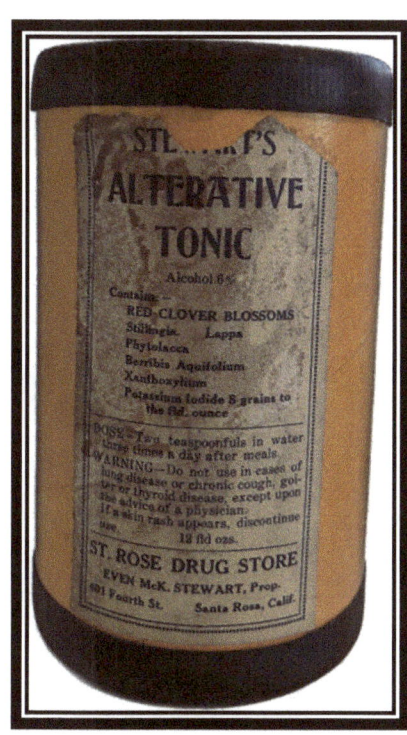

STEWART'S
ALTERATIVE
TONIC

Alcohol 6%

Contains:
RED CLOVER BLOSSOMS
Stillingia Lappa
Phytolacca
Berribis Aquifolium
Xanthoxylum
Potassium Iodide 5 grains to
the fld. ounce

ST. ROSE DRUG STORE
EVEN McK. STEWART, Prop.
401 Fourth St. Santa Rosa, Calif.

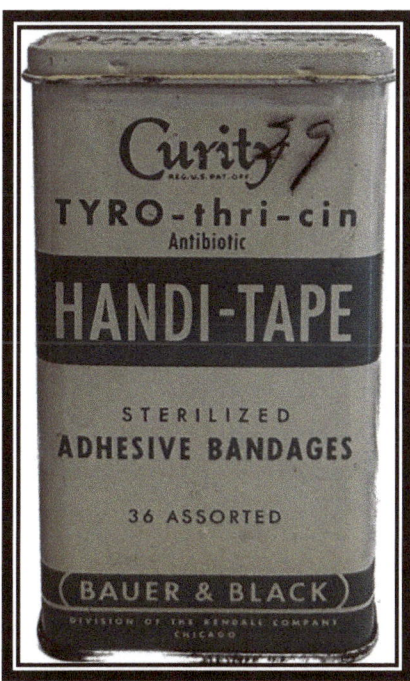

Curity
TYRO-thri-cin
Antibiotic
HANDI-TAPE
STERILIZED
ADHESIVE BANDAGES
36 ASSORTED
BAUER & BLACK
DIVISION OF THE KENDALL COMPANY
CHICAGO

MERCUROCHROME
MEDICATED
TO OPEN PRESS CAN - SLIDE COVER
HYGRADE
Waterproof
EMERGENCY
BANDAGES

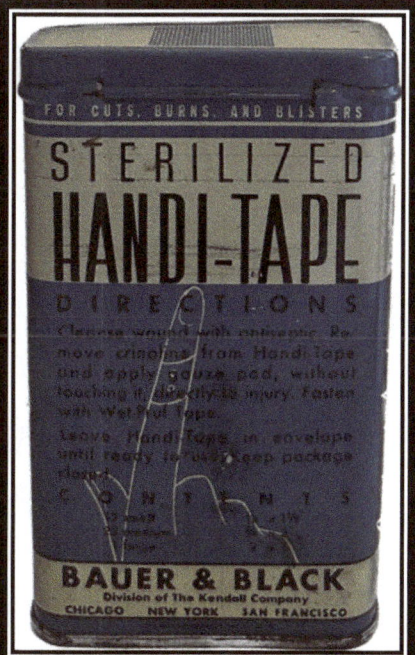

FOR CUTS, BURNS, AND BLISTERS
STERILIZED
HANDI-TAPE
DIRECTIONS
BAUER & BLACK
Division of The Kendall Company
CHICAGO NEW YORK SAN FRANCISCO

Additional druggist items

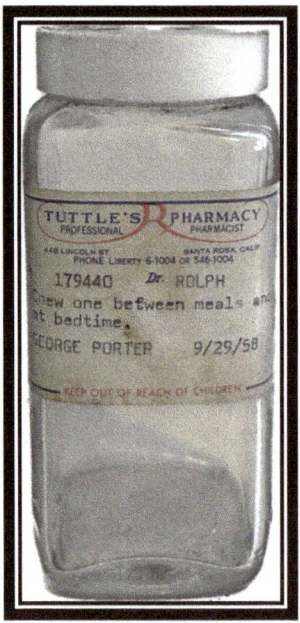

Rick Siri Collection

TWO CARNIVAL OF ROSES & ONE
NATIVE SONS OF THE GOLDEN WEST SOUVENIR BADGES

COURT EXCHANGE
SALOON AND CLUB ROOMS
Next to Hall of Records,
SANTA ROSA,   CALIFORNIA.
ED. NAGLE, Prop.

Howell & Bryant
DEALERS IN
GROCERIES, PROVISIONS, HAY,
GRAIN AND FEED, TEA, COF-
FEE, CIGARS AND TOBACCO.
ATHENAEUM BUILDING
SANTA ROSA, CAL.

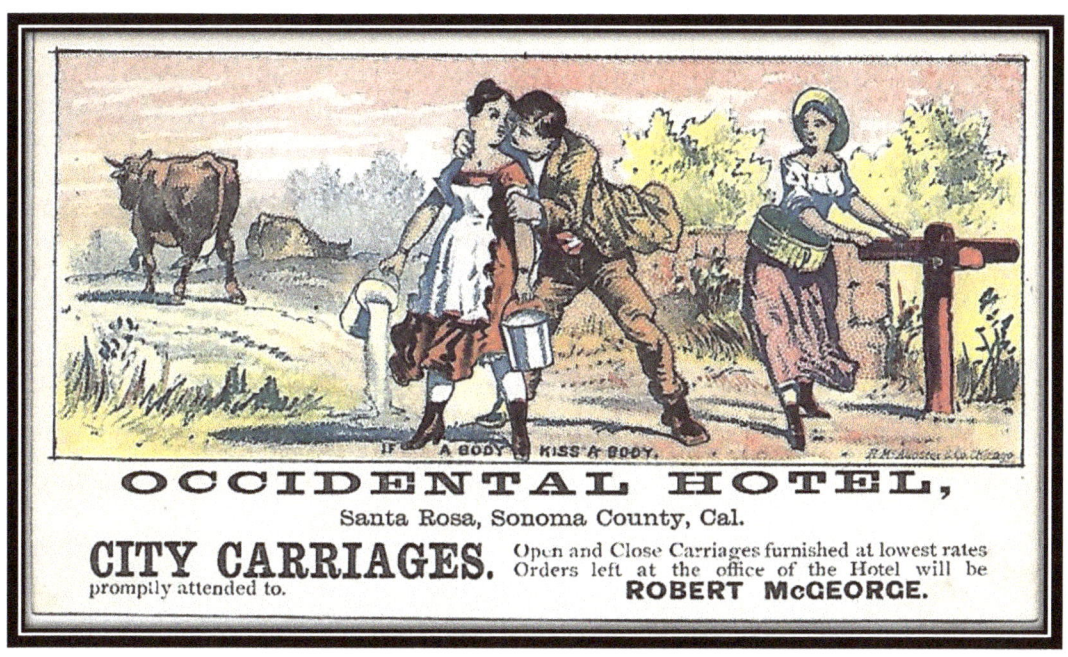

OCCIDENTAL HOTEL,

Santa Rosa, Sonoma County, Cal.

CITY CARRIAGES. Open and Close Carriages furnished at lowest rates Orders left at the office of the Hotel will be promptly attended to. ROBERT McGEORGE.

JAS. MORROW, Jr.,
Dealer in STOVES, TIN AND HARDWARE,
PUMPS, IRON AND LEAD PIPE, Etc.
195 Fourth St., opp. Hall of Records. SANTA ROSA, CAL.

E. A. SEEGELKEN,
Wholesale and Retail
DEALER IN
Groceries, Wines, Liquors,
TOBACCO AND CIGARS,
Corner Fourth and Wilson Streets,
SANTA ROSA, CAL.

E. A. SEEGELKEN,
Wholesale and Retail
DEALER IN
Groceries, Wines, Liquors,
TOBACCO AND CIGARS,
Corner Fourth and Wilson Streets,
SANTA ROSA, CAL.

E. A. SEEGELKEN,
Wholesale and Retail
DEALER IN
Groceries, Wines, Liquors,
TOBACCO AND CIGARS,
Corner Fourth and Wilson Streets,
SANTA ROSA, CAL.

GOING TO THE PLANTATION.

S. G. PALMER,
BOOT AND SHOE FACTORY
North Side of Plaza,
SANTA ROSA, CALIFORNIA.

NOON HOUR ON THE PLANTATION.

S. G. PALMER,
BOOT AND SHOE FACTORY
North Side of Plaza,
SANTA ROSA, CALIFORNIA.

Compliments of
S. H. MAUZY,
CASH
BOOT AND SHOE STORE,
PETALUMA, CAL.

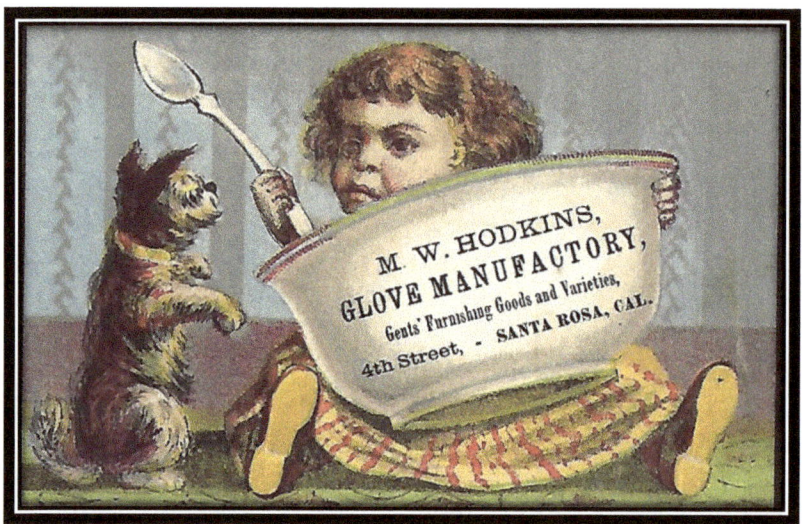

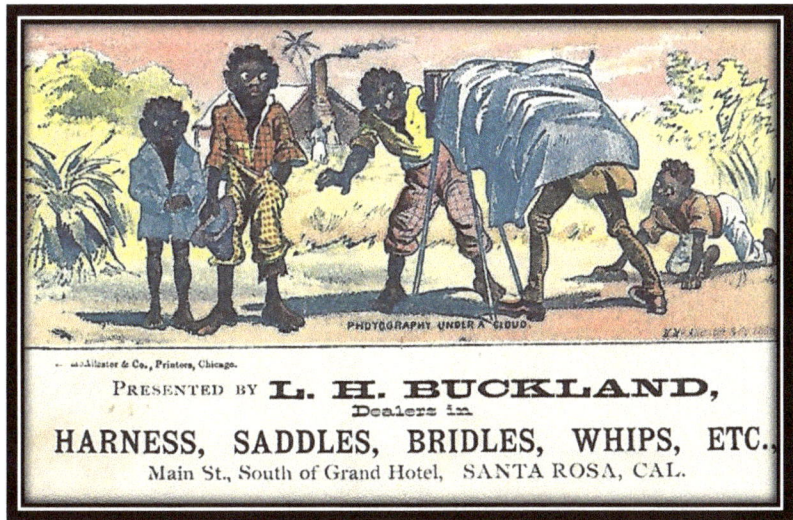

PRESENTED BY **L. H. BUCKLAND,**
Dealers in
HARNESS, SADDLES, BRIDLES, WHIPS, ETC.,
Main St., South of Grand Hotel, SANTA ROSA, CAL.

PRESENTED BY **L. H. BUCKLAND,**
Dealers in
HARNESS, SADDLES, BRIDLES, WHIPS, ETC.,
Main St., South of Grand Hotel, SANTA ROSA, CAL.

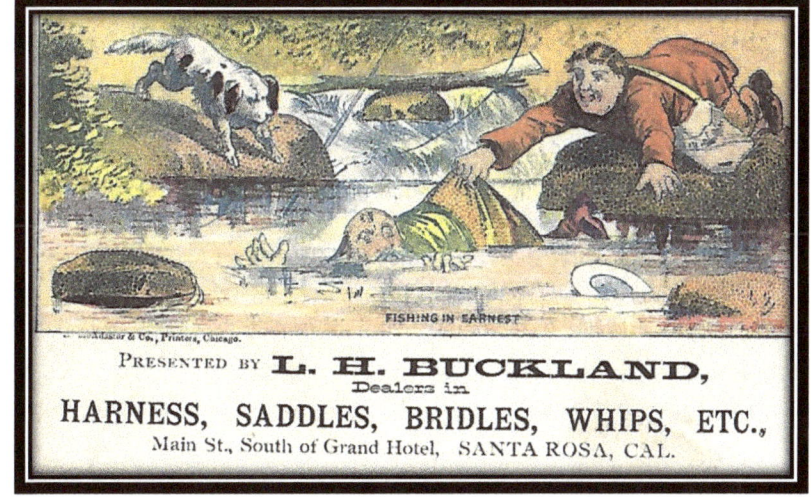

PRESENTED BY **L. H. BUCKLAND,**
Dealers in
HARNESS, SADDLES, BRIDLES, WHIPS, ETC.,
Main St., South of Grand Hotel, SANTA ROSA, CAL.

SPECIAL POCKET SAMPLE CASE

FROM

UNION CARD COMPANY

COLUMBUS, OHIO

DEALERS IN

ALL KINDS OF HIDDEN NAME CARDS, POST CARDS, ART PICTURES,
RINGS, JEWELRY, ETC,

ORDER THE CARDS BY THE NUMBER PRINTED ABOVE THEM

No. 148. New Envelope Card, (assorted designs) 12 for 20 cents
Name printed on card and enclosed in envelope

No. 149. "Variety Pack" (all different) with name, 12 for 15 cents

ORDER THE CARDS BY THE NUMBER PRINTED ABOVE THEM
No. 140. With name, (assorted scrap picture) 12 for 10 cents

ONE OF THE FASHION-PLATE ENSEMBLES
—IN—
VICTOR HERBERT'S OPERATIC TRIUMPH
"THE PRINCESS PAT"
BOOK AND LYRICS BY HENRY BLOSSOM

Winter is here, and so is
CORTICELLI SILK,
and we are all in our glory.

W. B. VEIRS,

→ DEALER IN ←

Dry and Fancy Goods, Clothing

HATS, BOOTS and SHOES, Etc.,

20 HINTON AVENUE,

NEXT TO CITY HALL.

SANTA ROSA, CAL.

JOHN O. DOANE & CO.

→ **ONE PRICE** ←

Dry Goods and Carpet House

CHAS. ROHRER.

Manager.

DEMOCRAT BUILDING,

SANTA ROSA,

CAL.

-   EDUCATION
Two Santa Rosa High School postcards & school class pin

Ursuline School near where St. Rose School is today

Ursuline High School 1906 class pin

Old Santa Rosa High School on Humboldt Street. Burned down in 1921.

Old Fremont Grammer School used as Santa Rosa High School Annex 1923.

Current Santa Rosa High School
Mendocino Avenue

Luther Burbank Grade School

**Fremont Grammar School on College Avenue
Currently Santa Rosa Middle School**

Santa Rosa Jr. College on Mendocino Avenue c. 1940's

Pacific Methodist College – Between McConnell & Beaver Streets c. 1891

Ursuline College next to St. Rose Church & School Santa Rosa

Ursuline College, Santa Rosa, Cal.

Ursuline College next to St. Rose Church Santa Rosa

Ursuline College Main Entrance

Ursuline College turn of the century

Sweets Business College Santa Rosa c. 1920's

Sweet's Santa Rosa Business College

Sweet's Santa Rosa Business College

Sweets Business College
Bottom Row Mary Maroni – Capitani 15th from the right

Marie Evelyn Maroni (Capitani)
Santa Rosa Business College Diploma

George DeForrest Barnell
Santa Rosa High School Diploma

CHURCHES

Left card First Christian Church
Next to Sweets Business College on Ross Street

Right card South Methodist Church
Left standing during & after 1906 Earthquake

Roman Catholic Church on B Street

Episcopal Church on Mendocino Avenue

Methodist Church downtown Santa Rosa c. 1919

Episcopal Church on Mendocino Avenue

View of three Santa Rosa Churches

First Baptist Church built from one Redwood Tree

HOTELS

Santa Rosa House
E. P. Colgan Proprietor, c.1850's

Western Hotel Lower Fourth Street

Face of Grand Hotel on Third Street

Full view of Grand Hotel

Overton Hotel Santa Rosa

Overton Hotel Advertisement

Occidental Hotel Santa Rosa on Fourth & B Streets view

Occidental Hotel Advertisement

Occidental Hotel Two Stories prior 1937
Corner 5ᵗʰ & B Streets view

Occidental Hotel Three Stories after 1937
Corner of 4ᵗʰ & B Streets view

Occidental Hotel above Keegan Bros. late 1940's early 1950's

Occidental Hotel across from Hardisty's on 4th & B Streets

Santa Rosa Hotel above Rosenburg's Department Store
Formerly the Overton Hotel

Later view of the Santa Rosa Hotel above The Fashion

Originally Santa Rosa Bank; then Bank of Italy; and then Bank of America
Now known as "The Empire Building"
Fourth & Exchange Avenue

Savings Bank of Santa Rosa corner Fourth & Exchange Avenue

Santa Rosa National Bank on Hinton Avenue

Exchange Bank on Fourth & Main (Mendocino) Avenue

Bank of Italy Advertisement later to be Bank of America

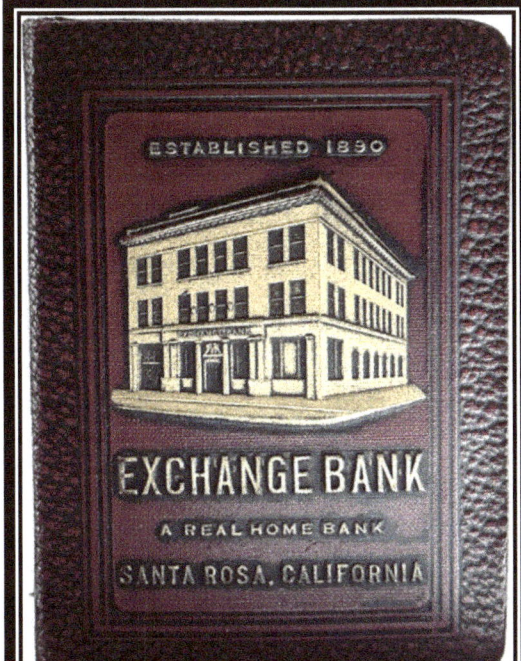

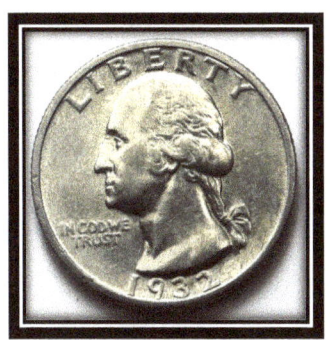

Exchange Bank Savings Coin Bank

Bank of Italy Check Book
Coinage during that era

Bank of Italy Savings Coin Bank

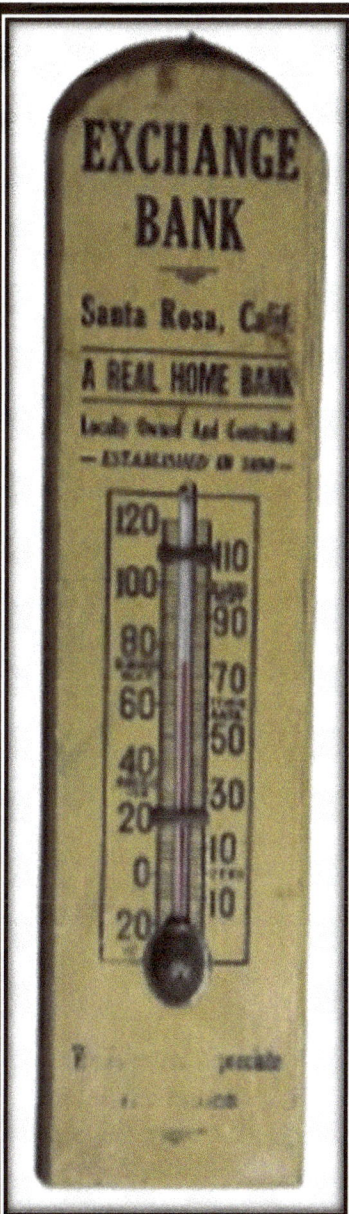

M. S. Spencer & Co.
West of Court House
1895

Reverse

1912 Calendar

Gallon Crock

Kopf & Donovan purchased the Frank Grace grocery store on the corners of 4th and A Streets in 1896.

P. Signorotti & A. Canevari
401 South A Street

THE moral of this, the Sixteenth Card of our Series, is that, if young ladies would avoid creating a scene, similar to **The Ghost Story!** the one the artist, Mr. R. W. Buss, gives us in this admirable picture, they had better forego reading ghost stories at bed-time.

As the rough, wintry season of the year approaches, do not forget that a **Cold**, once contracted, demands prompt treatment, lest the accompanying Cough should inflame and rack the Lungs, and induce the formation of tubercles. By the use of DR. JAYNE'S EXPECTORANT, in small doses,—repeating same according to the urgency of the symptoms,—your Cold will speedily yield, and your Lungs become a dangerous ordeal. If you should be seized with a Sore Throat, **Bronchitis**, or any **Bronchial Disorder**, the EXPECTORANT will subdue the inflammation of the parts, detach the mucous matter which clogs them, and gradually promote its removal. In case of **Asthma**, the EXPECTORANT overcomes the cause of the trouble, and a prompt restoration follows. If attacked by **Pleurisy**, or any **Acute Inflammation** of the Lungs or Throat, take the EXPECTORANT according to directions,—bathing the parts thoroughly with DR. JAYNE'S LINIMENT,—and covering up warmly in bed. The EXPECTORANT, if taken in quite small doses by **Consumptives**, will ameliorate the symptoms, and especially ease the Cough as well as the oppression and soreness of the Lungs and Throat. It is a helpful remedy also in cases of **Croup** and **Whooping-Cough**, checking the violence of the attacks, and relieving the attending distress.

A Trusty Family Tonic Is at the service of those possessing a bottle of DR. JAYNE'S TONIC VERMIFUGE. For the **Dyspepsia of Adults**, Indigestion, Sour Stomach, Oppression at the pit of the Stomach, and Low Spirits, it is an excellent remedy,—the bowels in such cases being kept open, when necessary, by DR. JAYNE'S SANATIVE PILLS. **Worms** in **Children** it destroys with certainty, removing them and the distressing symptoms to which they give rise. As a **Strengthening Tonic** for feeble, sickly children, it renews the appetite and rebuilds the general health, and it has a curative effect in the Fever and Ague of the young.

PRESENTED By.

B. BRESLAUER,
Santa Rosa, Sonoma Co.,
California.

THE MAJOR & KNAPP LITH CO N.Y.

Potero Yeast Bakery & Restaurant
H. Demeyz Proprietor
199 Fourth Street

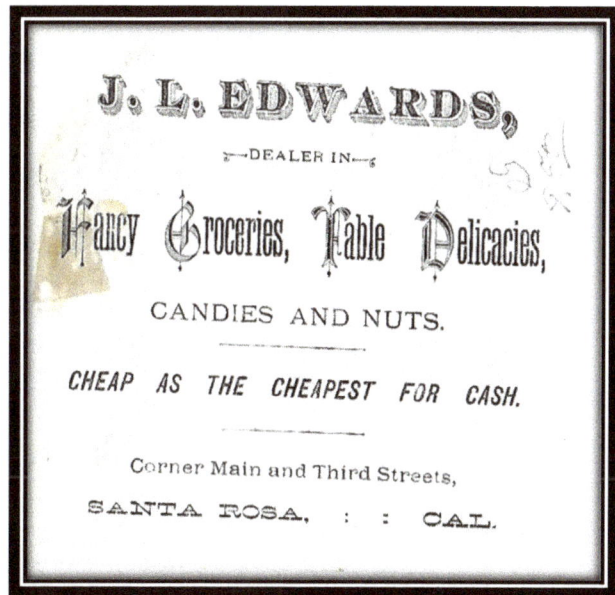

J. L. Edwards Fancy Groceries, Table Delicacies
Corner 3rd & Main Streets

LAVA
"Better Than a Turkish Bath"

Hand Wash Board

LOCAL RESTAURANTS

Hotel Overton Grill inside Hotel

Campi Restaurant on Fourth Street

Gallo Street Café on Sonoma Hi-Way East Santa Rosa

Hagel's Fine Food Restaurant Santa Rosa Avenue South

Topaz Lounge on Court House Square
Home of the 50 cent drink

Topaz Dining Room on Court House Square
Neil Blumenthal owner

Los Robles Lodge - Corner Cleveland & Edwards Avenue
Claus Neumann, owner

Flamingo Hotel Fourth & Farmers Lane
Built in 1957

Finest Accommodations
& food on Highway 101

RESTAURANT
COCKTAILS
COFFEE SHOP
QUEEN SIZE BEDS
PRIVATE LANAI WITH EVERY ROOM
SWIMMING POOLS
AIR CONDITIONED
OUTSIDE CATERING
COMPLETE BANQUET &
CONVENTION FACILITIES

HIGHWAY 101 NORTH AT STEELE LANE
SANTA ROSA, CALIFORNIA

LIBERTY 5-6330

Los Robles
LODGE

SANTA ROSA, CALIFORNIA

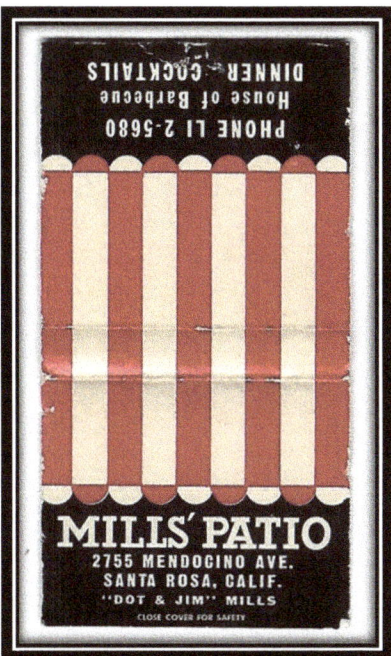

DINNER · COCKTAILS
House of Barbecue
PHONE LI 2-5680

MILLS' PATIO
2755 MENDOCINO AVE.
SANTA ROSA, CALIF.
"DOT & JIM" MILLS
CLOSE COVER FOR SAFETY

Your Friendly Host
NEIL B. BLUMENTHAL

542-7753

Topaz Room

SANTA ROSA · CALIFORNIA

CLOSE COVER BEFORE STRIKING MATCH

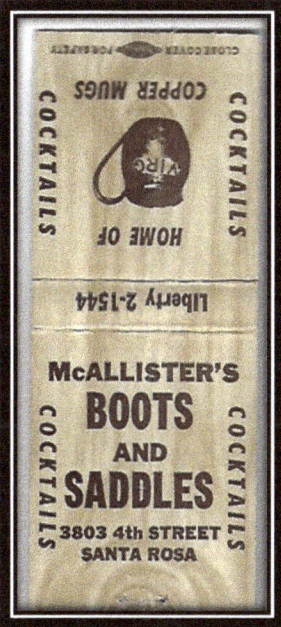

CLOSE COVER FOR SAFETY
COPPER MUGS
HOME OF
VFW
Liberty 2-1544

COCKTAILS   COCKTAILS

McALLISTER'S
BOOTS
AND
SADDLES

COCKTAILS   COCKTAILS

3803 4th STREET
SANTA ROSA

PALOMINO ROOM
for your favorite COCKTAILS
VISIT
OUR

LIBERTY 2-0975

SADDLE 'N
SIRLOIN

MONTGOMERY VILLAGE
SANTA ROSA, CALIFORNIA

4 Miles North Of
Santa Rosa, Calif.
Redwood Hwy. No.
4618
DANCING
ENTERTAINMENT
HOUSE OF FINE FOOD
Mary - Rico - Ed

Phone
Liberty 2-1721

Marco's

CLOSE COVER BEFORE STRIKING

"Made in the West for the West"
THREE GENERATIONS
OF FINE FOOD
Pianobar
Banquet Facilities
Dancing
Lunch - Dinner
Cocktails

Phone 542-5532

FAMOUS ITALIAN DINNERS

Lena's
WEST END VILLAGE
SANTA ROSA
"On the Sunset Side
of the Railroad Tracks"

Close Cover Before Striking Match

MOORE'S
T-BONE STEAKS & CHICKEN DINNERS
AND REAL BARBECUED MEATS
1/4 MILE SOUTH OF SANTA ROSA ON REDWOOD HIGHWAY
JACK MOORE, Prop.   Phone S. R. 2520

THE DIAMOND MATCH CO. N.Y.C.   CLOSE COVER BEFORE STRIKING MATCH

Phones LI 5-1766 LI 2-9924

Twin DRAGONS

Authentic
Chinese and American
Foods and Cocktails

640 - 3rd STREET
SANTA ROSA, CALIF.

CHOP SUEY

PHONE 1587

Jam-Kee Cafe
Chinese Food

Good Food

Virgil, Ida Tognozzi

**TOG'S
ITALIAN DINNERS**

655 SEBASTOPOL ROAD
ROSELAND VILLAGE
SANTA ROSA, CALIF.
Liberty 2-9923

CLOSE COVER FOR SAFETY

SANTA ROSA · CALIF.

Occidental
HOTEL
REMODELED AND
REFURNISHED 1937

**HOTEL
Occidental**

SANTA ROSA
CALIFORNIA

CLOSE COVER BEFORE STRIKING MATCH

A LA CARTE SERVICE
BUFFET
DINNERS
BREAKFASTS AND
SPECIAL LUNCHES

Featuring

**Santa Rosa
Cafe**

SINCE 1908
AT
440 4th STREET
PHONE 2280
SANTA ROSA, CALIF.

Close Cover Before

SUPERIOR MATCH CO., CHICAGO, U.S.A.

COFFEE
THAT
HITS THE
SPOT

Open All Night

**PAUL & ELSIE'S
LUNCH**

TASTY SANDWICHES
GOOD COFFEE

410 - 5th STREET
Opp. Post Office
SANTA ROSA, CALIF.

CLOSE COVER BEFORE STRIKING MATCH

HAMBURGERS
you'll LIKE

WE BAKE
OUR OWN
PIES

**GEORGE'S
LUNCH**

The Post Office Is
Opposite Us
410 - 5th St.
Santa Rosa, Calif.

CLOSE COVER BEFORE STRIKING

Liberty 5-9934

**SARA & JACK'S
HACIENDA**

3422 SANTA ROSA AVE.
3 Miles South of
SANTA ROSA, CALIF.

Close Cover For Safety

TANGUILLE ROOM

THE OHIO MATCH CO., SAN FRANCISCO, CAL.
MADE IN U.S.A.

Eisenhood's

FAMOUS
FOR FINE FOODS

· COURT HOUSE SQUARE · SANTA ROSA CALIF

CLOSE COVER BEFORE STRIKING

IRENE'S

MIXED DRINKS
SANDWICHES

108 ROBERTS AVE.
SANTA ROSA, CAL.

LI. 2-0861

Stein Haus
Hof Brau

1150 SANTA ROSA AVE.
SANTA ROSA, CALIF.

Good things

EAT HERE
and DIET HOME

LITTLE DINER

Ida Krause

★

408 MENDOCINO
SANTA ROSA, CALIF.
Phone LI. 5-9500

203 - 4th STREET
SANTA ROSA, CALIF.

★

MERCHANTS
LOWER 4th ST.
PROGRESSIVE
ONE OF THE

PHONE LI. 5-5163

BARREL HOUSE

"West of the Pecos"

★

COCKTAILS
MIXED DRINKS

Close Cover For Safety

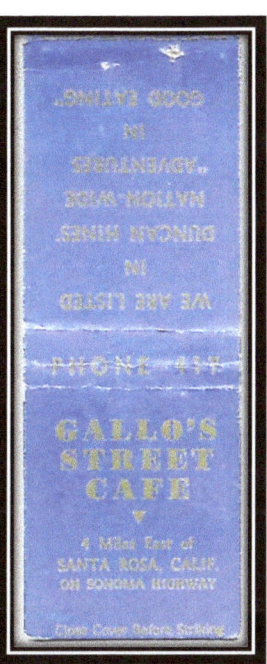

GALLO'S
STREET
CAFE

▼

4 Miles East of
SANTA ROSA, CALIF.
ON SONOMA HIGHWAY

Phone 3308
509 FOURTH STREET
SANTA ROSA,
CALIF.

WRIGHT'S
COFFEE SHOP

WRIGHT'S
COFFEE SHOP

Phone 3308

BREAKFAST
LUNCH
DINNER
FOUNTAIN SERVICE

43

HAMBURGERS you'll LIKE

A Good Place
TO EAT

DORY
SANDWICH SHOP

721 4th Street
SANTA ROSA, CALIF.

Across From
Rosenberg's Dept. Store

CLOSE COVER BEFORE STRIKING

Eisenhood's Fine Foods

● RESTAURANT
PHONE 1605

● DELICATESSEN
PHONE 238M

● DINING ROOM
● COFFEE SHOP
● COCKTAIL LOUNGE

● LIQUORS
● IMPORTS
● PREPARED FOODS

Court House Square   Montgomery Village

SANTA ROSA, CALIF.

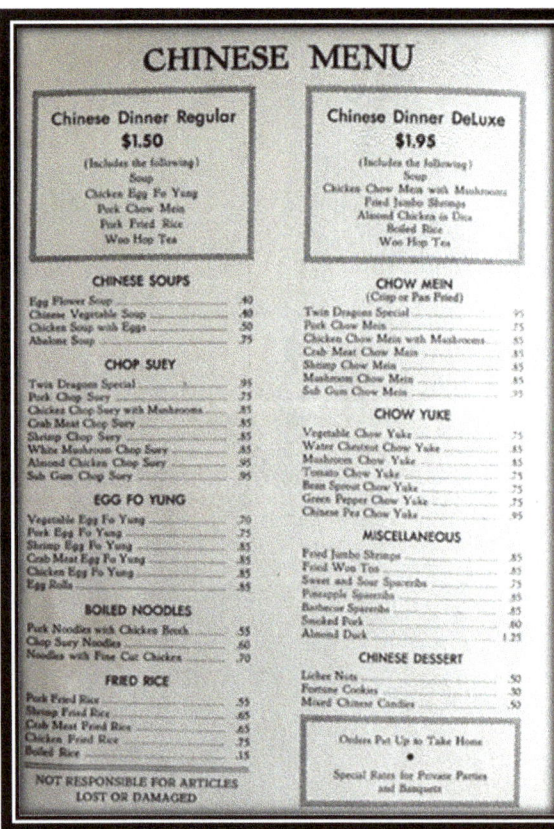

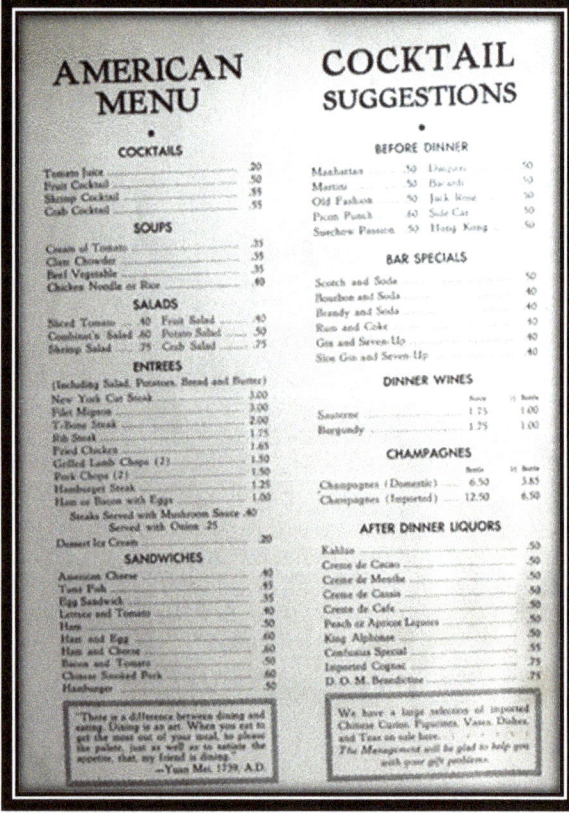

Twin Dragons Restaurant 640 Third Street
George & Bertha Yee opened Twin Dragon in the late 1930s

**Lena's Restaurant 509 Adams between West 6th & Adams Streets
Santa Rosa's favorite restaurant of the day**

Dance Request Card as seen on left top corner of left menu below

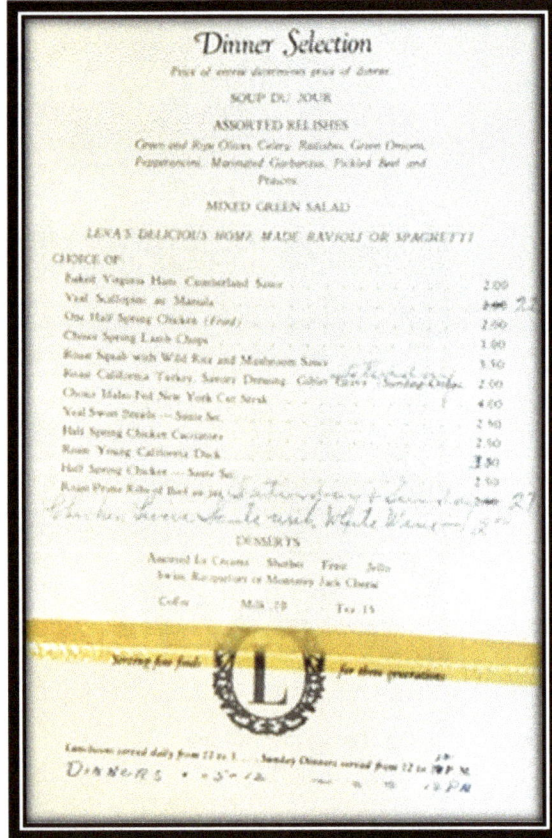

Lena's Night Club Restaurant Menu

Optimist Club member placing club meeting sign on building

Guidotti's Restaurant in background, later Michele's Restaurant

1945 Calendar

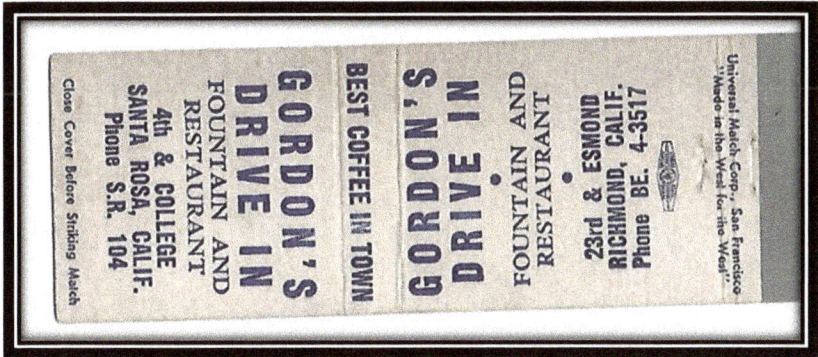

Santa Rosa's teenage hot spot

SANDWICHES

Hamburger - - - - - 35¢
COUNTRY STYLE 3-DECKER 55
CHEESEBURGER 40

Tenderized Steak Sandwich - 50¢
ON A BUN

Hot Turkey Sandwich, Giblet Gravy 80
Hot Beef or Pork Sandwich 75

Fish and Chips 60
ORDER OF FRENCH FRIES 20

50¢ BAR-B-QUE BEEF PORK 50¢

Fried Ham 45   Grilled Cheese 30
Ham or Bacon and Egg 55
Grilled Ham or Bacon and Cheese 55
Buttermilk 10

Three-Decker Sandwiches
Clubhouse   .   .   .   .   .   .   80¢
HAM AND CHEESE   .   .   .   .   65¢
BACON AND TOMATO   .   .   .   65¢
Above served with Potato Salad

Cold Sandwiches
Chicken Salad	40	Pork	45
Deviled Egg	30	Beef	45
Tomato and Lettuce	25	Ham	45
American Cheese	25	Turkey	60
Tuna Salad	40	Peanut Butter and Jelly	30

Buttered Sandwich 5¢ Extra   Grilled or Toasted Sandwich 5¢ Extra
Tomato on Sandwich 5¢ Extra

FOUNTAIN SERVICE

Milk Shakes 30
Malts 35
Hot Chocolate Malt, Floated with Ice Cream,
   Topped with Whipped Cream and a Cherry 30
Sodas 25
Floats 20
Sundaes — Marshmallow or Chocolate 35
Fresh Strawberry Sundae or Pineapple Sundae 40
Sundae with Hot Fudge 40
Sundae with Hot Caramel 40
Black and White Sundae 40
Ice Cream Dish 15
Freeze (any flavor) 25
Coke .... 10 & 15
Root Beer .... 10 & 15
Limeade .... 10 & 15
Lemonade 15
Orangeade 15
Grapeade 15

Shakes with Ice Cream 5¢ extra   Extra Scoop in Shakes 5¢ extra

Pie 20   Pie A la Mode 25   Donuts 10; (2) 15
Hot Apple Pie a la Mode 25

GORDON'S SPECIAL - - - - - 40¢
Toasted Almond Ice Cream with Caramel Topping,
Whipped Cream, Nuts and Cherry

BANANA SPLIT - - - - - - 45¢

Gordon's menu and classic 1956 Chevrolet

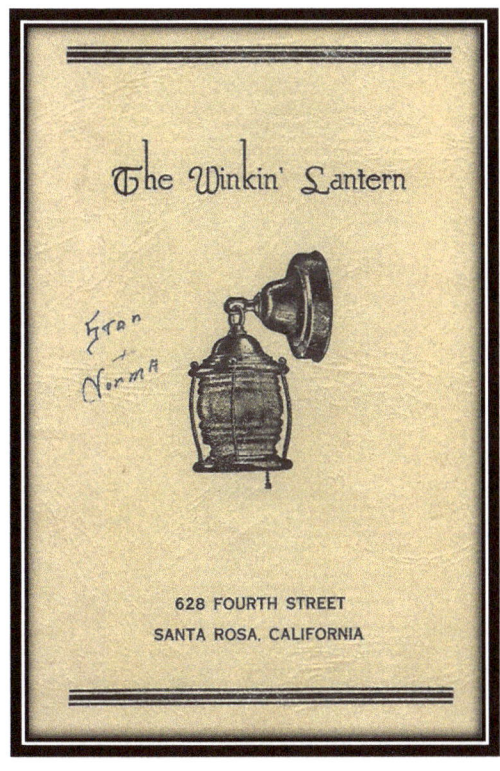

The Winkin' Lantern

628 FOURTH STREET
SANTA ROSA, CALIFORNIA

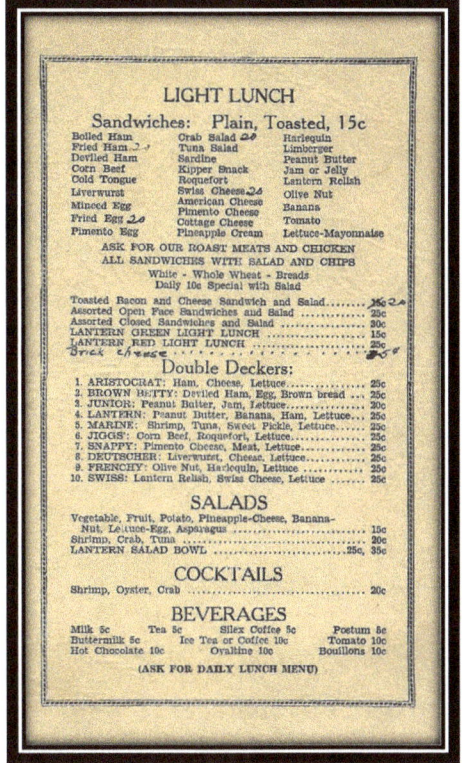

LIGHT LUNCH

Sandwiches: Plain, Toasted, 15c

Boiled Ham	Crab Salad 20	Harlequin
Fried Ham 20	Tuna Salad	Limberger
Deviled Ham	Sardine	Peanut Butter
Corn Beef	Kipper Snack	Jam or Jelly
Cold Tongue	Roquefort	Lantern Relish
Liverwurst	Swiss Cheese 20	Olive Nut
Minced Egg	American Cheese	Banana
Fried Egg 20	Pimento Cheese	Tomato
Pimento Egg	Cottage Cheese	Lettuce-Mayonnaise
	Pineapple Cream	

ASK FOR OUR ROAST MEATS AND CHICKEN
ALL SANDWICHES WITH SALAD AND CHIPS
White - Whole Wheat - Breads
Daily 10c Special with Salad

Toasted Bacon and Cheese Sandwich and Salad........ 20c
Assorted Open Face Sandwiches and Salad 20c
Assorted Closed Sandwiches and Salad 30c
LANTERN GREEN LIGHT LUNCH 15c
LANTERN RED LIGHT LUNCH 20c
Brick cheese 25c

Double Deckers:

1. ARISTOCRAT: Ham, Cheese, Lettuce 20c
2. BROWN BETTY: Deviled Ham, Egg, Brown bread ... 25c
3. JUNIOR: Peanut Butter, Jam, Lettuce........... 20c
4. LANTERN: Peanut Butter, Banana, Ham, Lettuce.. 25c
5. MARINE: Shrimp, Tuna, Sweet Pickle, Lettuce... 25c
6. JIGGS': Corn Beef, Roquefort, Lettuce......... 25c
7. SNAPPY: Pimento Cheese, Meat, Lettuce......... 25c
8. DEUTSCHER: Liverwurst, Cheese, Lettuce........ 25c
9. FRENCHY: Olive Nut, Harlequin, Lettuce........ 25c
10. SWISS: Lantern Relish, Swiss Cheese, Lettuce.. 25c

SALADS

Vegetable, Fruit, Potato, Pineapple-Cheese, Banana-
Nut, Lettuce-Egg, Asparagus 15c
Shrimp, Crab, Tuna 20c
LANTERN SALAD BOWL 25c, 35c

COCKTAILS

Shrimp, Oyster, Crab 20c

BEVERAGES

Milk 5c	Tea 5c	Silex Coffee 5c	Postum 5c
Buttermilk 5c	Ice Tea or Coffee 10c	Tomato 10c
Hot Chocolate 10c	Ovaltine 10c	Bouillon 10c

(ASK FOR DAILY LUNCH MENU)

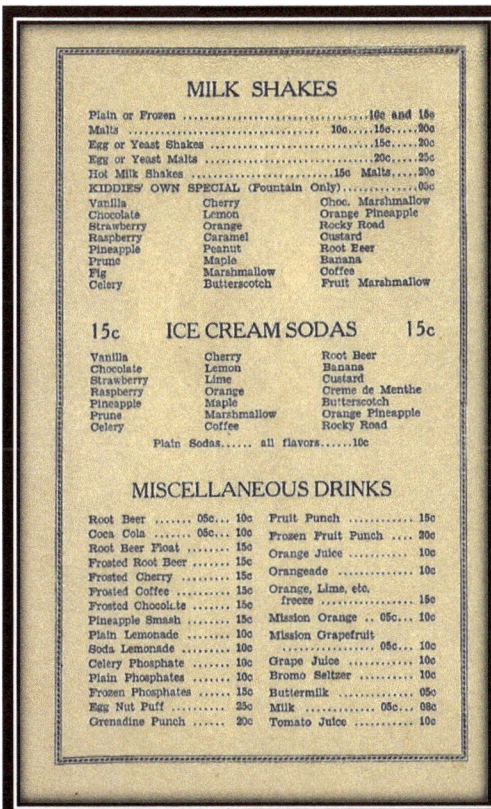

MILK SHAKES

Plain or Frozen ....10c and 15c
Malts ....10c....15c....20c
Egg or Yeast Shakes ....15c....20c
Egg or Yeast Malts ....20c....25c
Hot Milk Shakes ....15c Malts.....20c
KIDDIES' OWN SPECIAL (Fountain Only).............05c

Vanilla	Cherry	Choc. Marshmallow
Chocolate	Lemon	Orange Pineapple
Strawberry	Orange	Rocky Road
Raspberry	Caramel	Custard
Pineapple	Peanut	Root Beer
Prune	Maple	Banana
Fig	Marshmallow	Coffee
Celery	Butterscotch	Fruit Marshmallow

15c   ICE CREAM SODAS   15c

Vanilla	Cherry	Root Beer
Chocolate	Lemon	Banana
Strawberry	Lime	Custard
Raspberry	Orange	Creme de Menthe
Pineapple	Maple	Butterscotch
Prune	Marshmallow	Orange Pineapple
Celery	Coffee	Rocky Road

Plain Sodas...... all flavors....10c

MISCELLANEOUS DRINKS

Root Beer .... 05c... 10c	Fruit Punch 15c
Coca Cola .... 05c... 10c	Frozen Fruit Punch 20c
Root Beer Float 15c	Orange Juice 10c
Frosted Root Beer 15c	Orangeade 10c
Frosted Cherry 15c	Orange, Lime, etc.
Frosted Coffee 15c	freeze 15c
Frosted Chocolate 15c	Mission Orange .. 05c... 10c
Pineapple Smash 15c	Mission Grapefruit
Plain Lemonade 10c	.... 05c... 10c
Soda Lemonade 10c	Grape Juice 10c
Celery Phosphate 10c	Bromo Seltzer 10c
Plain Phosphates 10c	Buttermilk 05c
Frozen Phosphates 15c	Milk .... 05c... 08c
Egg Nut Puff 25c	Tomato Juice 10c
Grenadine Punch 20c	

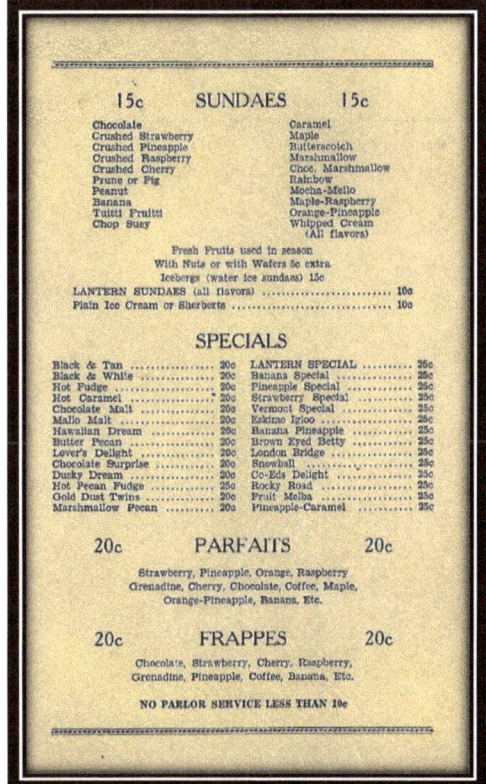

15c   SUNDAES   15c

Chocolate	Caramel
Crushed Strawberry	Maple
Crushed Pineapple	Butterscotch
Crushed Raspberry	Marshmallow
Crushed Cherry	Choc. Marshmallow
Prune or Fig	Rainbow
Peanut	Mocha-Mello
Banana	Maple-Raspberry
Tuitti Fruitti	Orange-Pineapple
Chop Suey	Whipped Cream
	(All flavors)

Fresh Fruits used in season
With Nuts or with Wafers 5c extra.
Icebergs (water ice sundaes) 15c
LANTERN SUNDAES (all flavors) 10c
Plain Ice Cream or Sherberts 10c

SPECIALS

Black & Tan 20c	LANTERN SPECIAL 25c
Black & White 20c	Banana Special 25c
Hot Fudge 20c	Pineapple Special 25c
Hot Caramel 20c	Strawberry Special 25c
Chocolate Malt 20c	Vermont Special 25c
Mallo Malt 20c	Eskimo Igloo 25c
Hawaiian Dream 20c	Banana Pineapple 25c
Butter Pecan 20c	Brown Eyed Betty 25c
Lover's Delight 20c	London Bridge 25c
Chocolate Surprise 20c	Snowball 25c
Ducky Dream 20c	Co-Eds Delight 25c
Hot Pecan Fudge 25c	Rocky Road 25c
Gold Dust Twins 20c	Fruit Melba 25c
Marshmallow Pecan 20c	Pineapple-Caramel 25c

20c   PARFAITS   20c

Strawberry, Pineapple, Orange, Raspberry,
Grenadine, Cherry, Chocolate, Coffee, Maple,
Orange-Pineapple, Banana, Etc.

20c   FRAPPES   20c

Chocolate, Strawberry, Cherry, Raspberry,
Grenadine, Pineapple, Coffee, Banana, Etc.

NO PARLOR SERVICE LESS THAN 10c

COURT HOUSE SQUARE
SANTA ROSA

*"An Ideal Menu Is Not One of Many Things,
But of Choice Ones"*

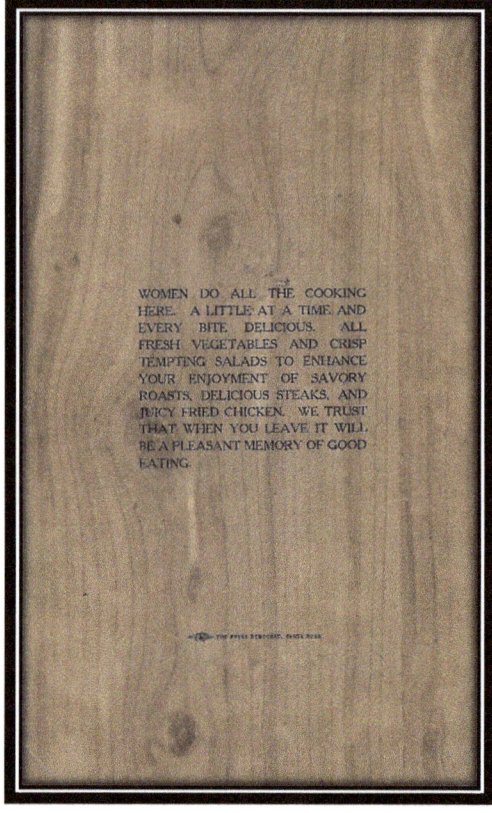

WOMEN DO ALL THE COOKING HERE. A LITTLE AT A TIME AND EVERY BITE DELICIOUS. ALL FRESH VEGETABLES AND CRISP TEMPTING SALADS TO ENHANCE YOUR ENJOYMENT OF SAVORY ROASTS, DELICIOUS STEAKS, AND JUICY FRIED CHICKEN. WE TRUST THAT WHEN YOU LEAVE IT WILL BE A PLEASANT MEMORY OF GOOD EATING.

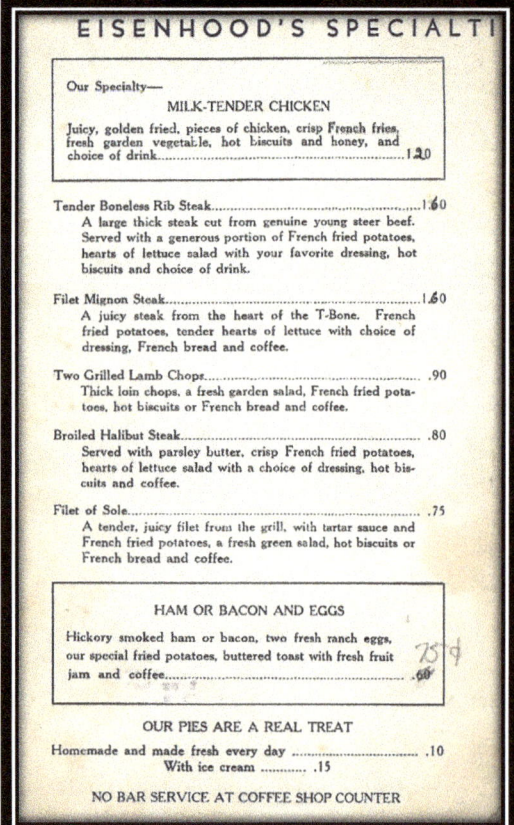

EISENHOOD'S SPECIALTIES SERVED AT ANY TIME

Our Specialty—
MILK-TENDER CHICKEN
Juicy, golden fried, pieces of chicken, crisp French fries, fresh garden vegetable, hot biscuits and honey, and choice of drink..........1.20

Tender Boneless Rib Steak..........1.60
A large thick steak cut from genuine young steer beef. Served with a generous portion of French fried potatoes, hearts of lettuce salad with your favorite dressing, hot biscuits and choice of drink.

Filet Mignon Steak..........1.60
A juicy steak from the heart of the T-Bone. French fried potatoes, tender hearts of lettuce with choice of dressing, French bread and coffee.

Two Grilled Lamb Chops..........90
Thick loin chops, a fresh garden salad, French fried potatoes, hot biscuits or French bread and coffee.

Broiled Halibut Steak..........80
Served with parsley butter, crisp French fried potatoes, hearts of lettuce salad with a choice of dressing, hot biscuits and coffee.

Filet of Sole..........75
A tender, juicy filet from the grill, with tartar sauce and French fried potatoes, a fresh green salad, hot biscuits or French bread and coffee.

HAM OR BACON AND EGGS
Hickory smoked ham or bacon, two fresh ranch eggs, our special fried potatoes, buttered toast with fresh fruit jam and coffee..........60

OUR PIES ARE A REAL TREAT
Homemade and made fresh every day..........10
With ice cream..........15

NO BAR SERVICE AT COFFEE SHOP COUNTER

Our Special—
CLUB SANDWICH
A three deck toasted sandwich, with breast of chicken, crisp bacon, sliced tomatoes, lettuce and mayonnaise..........60

Eisenhood Special—
A three deck toasted sandwich, with sliced ham, cheese, tomatoes, crisp lettuce and mayonnaise..........50

PLAIN SANDWICHES
Buttered whole wheat, white or rye bread

Ham and Egg	.35
Sliced Breast of Chicken	.35
Pure Ground Beef Hamburger De Luxe	.25
Pure Ground Beef Hamburger	.20
Denver on Toast	.35
Fresh Deviled Egg	.20
Tuna Fish	.25
American or Swiss Cheese	.20
Fried Egg in Butter	.20
Sliced Tomato and Lettuce	.20
American Sardine	.20
Toasted Melted Cheese	.20
Peanut Butter	.20
Fried Hickory Smoked Ham	.30
Ham and Cheese	.30
Crisp Bacon and Tomato	.30
Fresh Fruit Jelly	.20
Special Plain Ham	.25
Grilled Cheeseburger	.25
Hot Beef or Pork (with potatoes and gravy)	.35

REFRESHING SALADS
(served with wafers)

Fresh Combination Vegetable Salad..........50
Our special blend of garden vegetables served with Thousand Island or French dressing.

Fruit Salad..........50
A select choice of fruit topped with a cream mayonnaise dressing.

Health Salad..........50
Creamy cottage cheese with pineapple slices and special dressing. Low in calories.

Fresh Shrimp or Crab Salad..........60
A delicious salad, served with Louie Dressing.

Hearts of Lettuce..........20
Served with your favorite dressing

Our Special..........60
Combination garden vegetable salad topped with sea food, and a special dressing

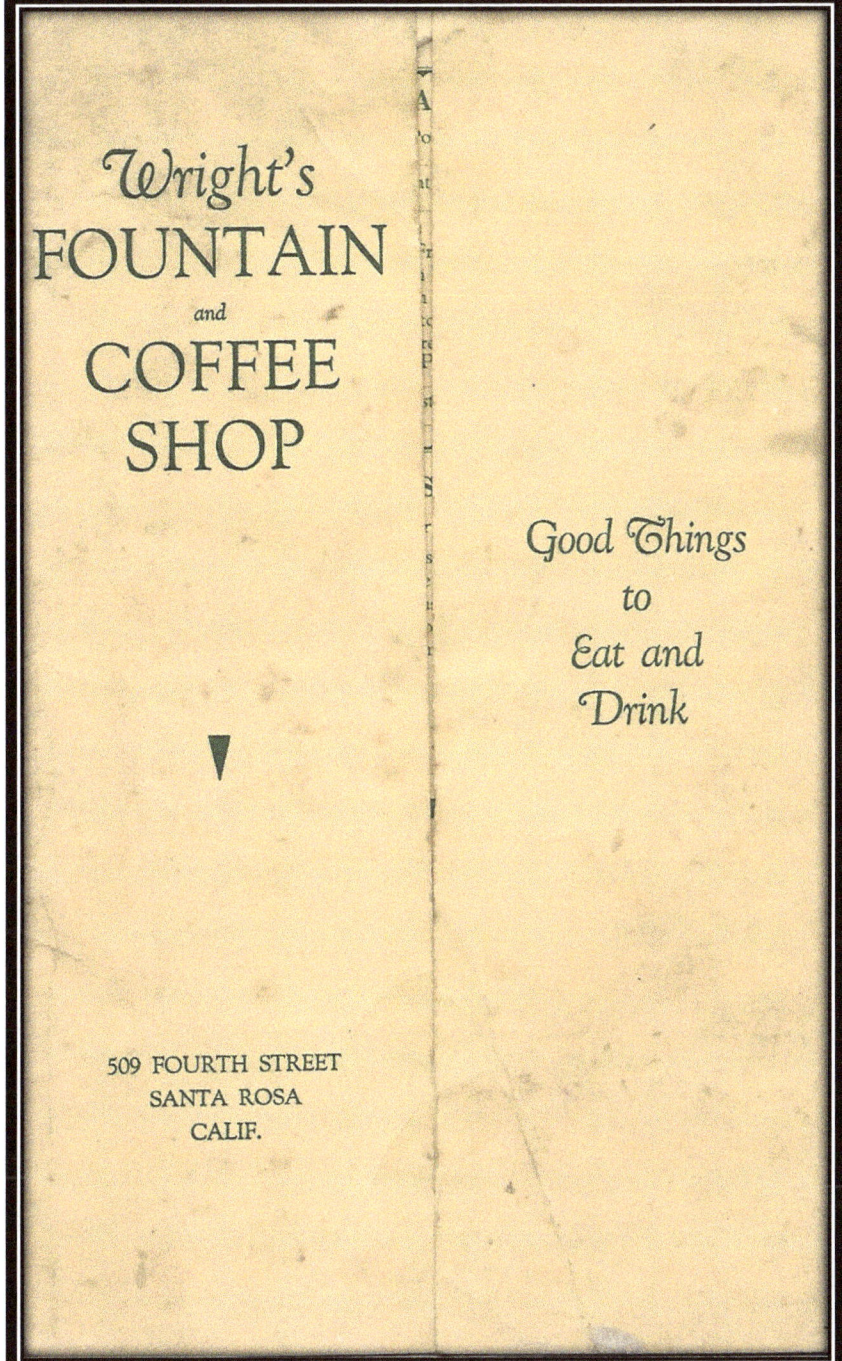

Wright's
FOUNTAIN
and
COFFEE
SHOP

▼

509 FOURTH STREET
SANTA ROSA
CALIF.

*Good Things
to
Eat and
Drink*

FOUNTAIN SPECIALS

Jumbo Ice Cream Sodas, all flavors	.25
Milk Shakes, all flavors	.25
Malted Milks	.30
Egg Malted Milk	.35
Ice Cream, all flavors	.15
Sherbets	.15
Root Beer Float	.20
Frosted Root Beer	.20

PLAIN SUNDAES

Fresh Strawberry	.30
Chocolate, Crushed Pineapple or Marshmallow	.30
With Chopped Nuts	.35

FANCY SUNDAES

Coney Island	.40
Banana Special	.35
Pineapple Special	.40
Hot Butterscotch	.30
Frosted Donut Sundae	.20
Hot Caramel Sundae	.30
Hot Fudge	.30

FRUIT JUICES

Orange Juice	.15	.25
Pineapple Juice	.15	.25
Tomato Juice	.15	.25
Grapefruit Juice	.15	.25

PASTRY OR CAKE

Home Made Pies, (our own)	.15	.20
Pie a la Mode	.20	.25
Donut a la Mode		.15
Donut Shortcake in season		.25
Fruits in Season with Cream		.25
Plain or Sugared Donuts and Coffee		.19
Frosted Donuts and Coffee		.20

DRINKS

Pot of Tea	.10
Postum	.10
Coffee	.10
Bottle of Milk	.10
Buttermilk	.10
Hot Chocolate	.15

THREE-DECKER SANDWICHES

Grilled or Toasted

CLUB SANDWICH: Turkey, Bacon, Tomato .65

WRIGHT'S SPECIAL: Grilled Ham, Cheese and Tomato .40

ROYAL: Tuna, Deviled Egg, Lettuce, Chopped Olives and Mayonnaise .40

BURBANK: Consisting of Ham and Cheese dipped in Egg and Fried .45

HAWAIIAN: Consisting of Fried Ham, Sliced Pineapple on Toasted Bun .45

SANDWICHES

Plain, Toasted or Grilled

Choice of White, Whole Wheat, Rye or Raisin Bread

Hamburger (ground round) Sandwich	.25
Cheeseburger (ground round)	.30
Ham and Egg Sandwich	.40
Fried Ham Sandwich	.35
Fried Egg Sandwich	.30
Bacon and Tomato Sandwich	.35
Liverwurst Sandwich	.30
Tuna Salad Sandwich	.30
Lettuce and Tomato Sandwich	.25
Peanut Butter and Jelly Sandwich	.25
Cold Ham Sandwich	.30
Pimento Cheese Sandwich	.25
Cold Beef or Pork Sandwich	.35
American or Swiss Cheese Sandwich	.25
Minced Olive Sandwich	.25
Deviled Egg Sandwich	.25
Denver Sandwich	.40
Cold Sliced Turkey Sandwich	.50
Side Order French Fries	.15

SPECIALTIES

Club Filet Steak with French Fried Potatoes	$1.50
New York Steak	1.50
Top Sirloin Steak, French Fried Potatoes	1.50
Pork Chops, French Fried Potatoes	1.00
Lamb Chops, French Fried Potatoes	1.00
Half Fried Chicken with Salad and French Fried Potatoes	1.00
Hamburger Steak with Salad, French Fried Potatoes	.75
Ham and Eggs, Potatoes, Toast, Jam and Coffee	.75
Hot Roast Beef Sandwich with Potatoes and Gravy	.50
Hamburger Special Sandwich with French Fried Potatoes, Sherbet	.45
French Fried Shrimps, French Fried Potatoes	.90
Breaded Veal Cutlets	1.00
Ham Steak and Eggs, Potatoes, Toast and Coffee	1.00
Hot Turkey Sandwich	.65

BREAKFAST SUGGESTIONS

Please Order by Number

1. Choice of Dry Cereal and Two Eggs (any style), Toast and Coffee	.60
2. Country Fresh Eggs, (2), any style, Toast, Coffee and Potatoes	.45
3. Ham and Eggs with Potatoes, Toast, Jam and Coffee	.75
4. Bacon and Eggs with Potatoes, Toast, Jam and Coffee	.75
5. Omelette with Choice of Jelly, Tomato, Cheese or Ham	.60

Plain Omelette	.40	Side Order of Eggs (2)	.25
Griddle Cakes	.25	Side Order Ham, Bacon, Sausage	.35
Buckwheat Cakes			.30
Grapefruit, Peaches, Pears, Applesauce, or Prunes			.20
Choice of Dry Cereal with Cream			.25

WAFFLES

Creamed Waffle with Butter and Syrup	.25
Fresh Strawberry Waffle with Whipped Cream	.50
Waffle, Striped with Bacon, Ham or Sausage	.55
Walnut Waffle with Butter and Syrup	.35

SALADS

Combination Vegetable Salad Bowl with Toast	.45
Chilled Fruit Salad Bowl with Whipped Cream and Raisin Toast	.45
Pineapple or Peach with Cottage Cheese	.40
Lettuce and Tomato Salad	.30
Potato Salad	.30

•

NO FOUNTAIN SERVICE IN BOOTHS DURING LUNCH OR DINNER HOURS EXCEPT WITH MEALS

OWING TO PRESENT CONDITIONS WE MUST RESERVE BOOTHS FOR TWO OR MORE

Minimum Service per Person in Booths .10

Not responsible for lost articles

Wright's Fountain Menu

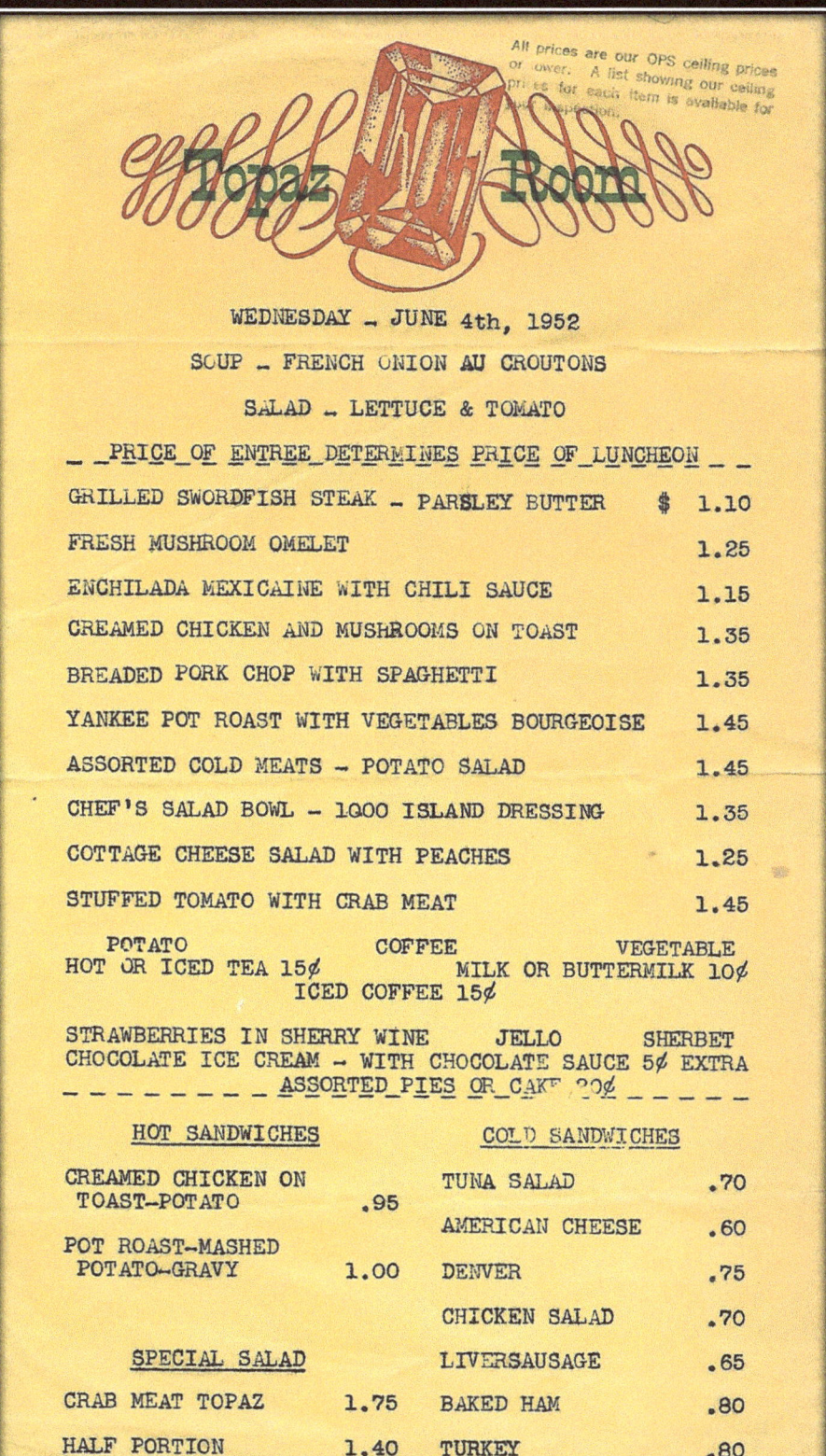

Topaz Room

WEDNESDAY – JUNE 4th, 1952

SOUP – FRENCH ONION AU CROUTONS

SALAD – LETTUCE & TOMATO

_ _PRICE_OF_ENTREE_DETERMINES_PRICE_OF_LUNCHEON_ _ _

GRILLED SWORDFISH STEAK – PARSLEY BUTTER	$ 1.10
FRESH MUSHROOM OMELET	1.25
ENCHILADA MEXICAINE WITH CHILI SAUCE	1.15
CREAMED CHICKEN AND MUSHROOMS ON TOAST	1.35
BREADED PORK CHOP WITH SPAGHETTI	1.35
YANKEE POT ROAST WITH VEGETABLES BOURGEOISE	1.45
ASSORTED COLD MEATS – POTATO SALAD	1.45
CHEF'S SALAD BOWL – 1000 ISLAND DRESSING	1.35
COTTAGE CHEESE SALAD WITH PEACHES	1.25
STUFFED TOMATO WITH CRAB MEAT	1.45

POTATO   COFFEE   VEGETABLE
HOT OR ICED TEA 15¢   MILK OR BUTTERMILK 10¢
ICED COFFEE 15¢

STRAWBERRIES IN SHERRY WINE   JELLO   SHERBET
CHOCOLATE ICE CREAM – WITH CHOCOLATE SAUCE 5¢ EXTRA
_ _ _ _ _ _ _ _ _ ASSORTED_PIES_OR_CAKE 20¢ _ _ _ _ _ _

HOT SANDWICHES		COLD SANDWICHES	
CREAMED CHICKEN ON TOAST–POTATO	.95	TUNA SALAD	.70
		AMERICAN CHEESE	.60
POT ROAST–MASHED POTATO–GRAVY	1.00	DENVER	.75
		CHICKEN SALAD	.70
SPECIAL SALAD		LIVERSAUSAGE	.65
CRAB MEAT TOPAZ	1.75	BAKED HAM	.80
HALF PORTION	1.40	TURKEY	.80

1952 Topaz Room Menu

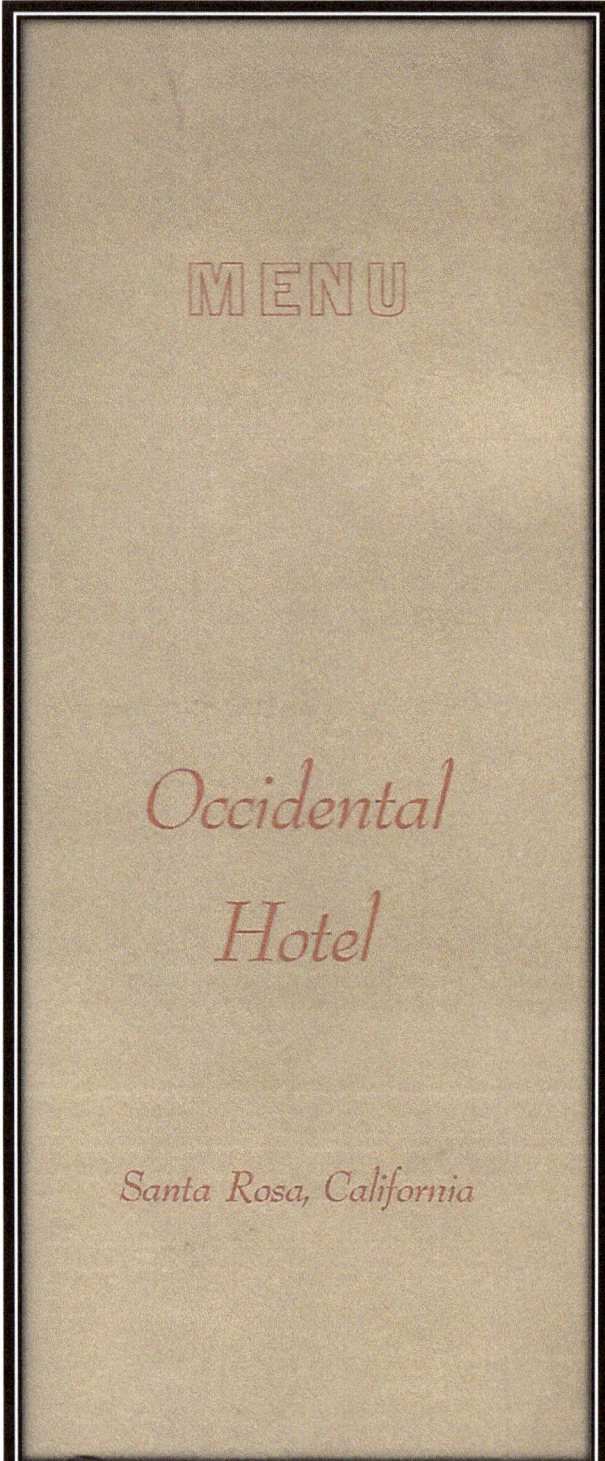

MENU

Occidental

Hotel

Santa Rosa, California

Appetizers

Marinated Herring with Sour Cream	.50
Fresh Fruit Cocktail Supreme	.60
Shrimp Cocktail Supreme	.80
Crab or Lobster Cocktail Supreme	.80
Half Sherried Grapefruit	.30
Celery Hearts and Jumbo Olives	.45
Tomato Juice Cocktail	.25
Smoked Salmon	.65
Assorted Cheese and Sea Food Canapies	.50
Relish Tray Occidental 50c for one, 25c for each additional person.	
Any Small Sea Food or Fruit Cocktail	.40

Salads

Hearts of Lettuce .45 . . . Half Order	.25
Sliced Chilled Tomatoes .45 . Half Order	.25
Combination Salad	.85
Shrimp or Crab .90 . . . a la Louie	1.25
Half Avocado Sliced	.35
Avocado Salad Occidental	.65
Chef's Green Salad Bowl	.60
Chef's Green Salad Bowl, Meat & Fowl Garnish	.85
Chef's Green Salad Bowl, Sea Food Garnish	.85
Shredded Lettuce, Tomatoes, Anchovies	.75
California Fruit Salad Plate, Cottage Cheese	.90
Chicken Salad	.80
Tuna Salad	.70
Cole Slaw	.25

Soups

Consomme, Clear	.25
Clam Chowder, Pismo	.25
Chicken Broth with Rice	.25
Soup du jour Cup .15 . . . Bowl	.25

Vegetables

Asparagus	.35
Fresh Carrots	.20
Stewed Tomatoes, Hot or Cold	.25
French Fried Onions	.35
Corn Off The Cob	.25
Corn On The Cob (in season)	.30
Fresh Button Mushrooms, Saute 1.00	
Half Order	.50

Hotel Dinner Menu

Sea Foods

Deep Fried Prawns, Hot Sauce	1.25
Fried Filet of Sole, Sauce Tartare	1.25
Fried Breaded Eastern Rock Scallops	1.25
Pan Fried Mountain Trout (2)	1.50
Broiled Half Lobster, Drawn Butter (in season)	1.75
Lobster Thermidor	2.00
Eastern Scallops, Poulette	1.50
Fried Eastern Oysters (in season)	1.25

Steaks and Chops

Eastern Loin Pork Chops, Apple Sauce	1.60
Prime Loin Lamb Chops (2)	2.00
Chef's Special Chopped Sirloin Steak, au jus	1.45
Choice Steer Top Sirloin Steak (12oz)	2.50
Choice Steer New York Cut Sirloin Steak (12-14 oz)	3.00
Filet Mignon (12oz)	3.25

New York Cut (For 2) . . 5.50

Filet Mignon Chateaubriand (For 2) . 6.00

Poultry

Chicken In Cream With Mushroom a la King, Casserole	1.35
Roast Young Turkey, Dressing and Cranberry Sauce	1.50
Southern Fried Half Chicken (unjointed)	1.65
Spring Chicken Saute au sec	1.85
Spring Chicken Saute a la Marengo, en Casserole	1.85

Specialties

Breaded Veal Cutlets, Cream Gravy	1.40
Chicken Liver Omelette	1.30
Spanish Omelette	.85
Cheddar Cheese Omelette	.75
Fresh Mushroom Omelette	1.50
Vegetable Plate With Poached Egg	1.00
Chef's Special Tenderloin Steak Sandwich	1.50

All the above prices are for a la Carte Service and include appropriate Potatoes, Rolls and Butter only. Any item will be served as an entree on a Complete Dinner with all accompaniments shown on the Daily Menu for an additional cost of 50c per person.

Occidental Hotel Dinner Menu

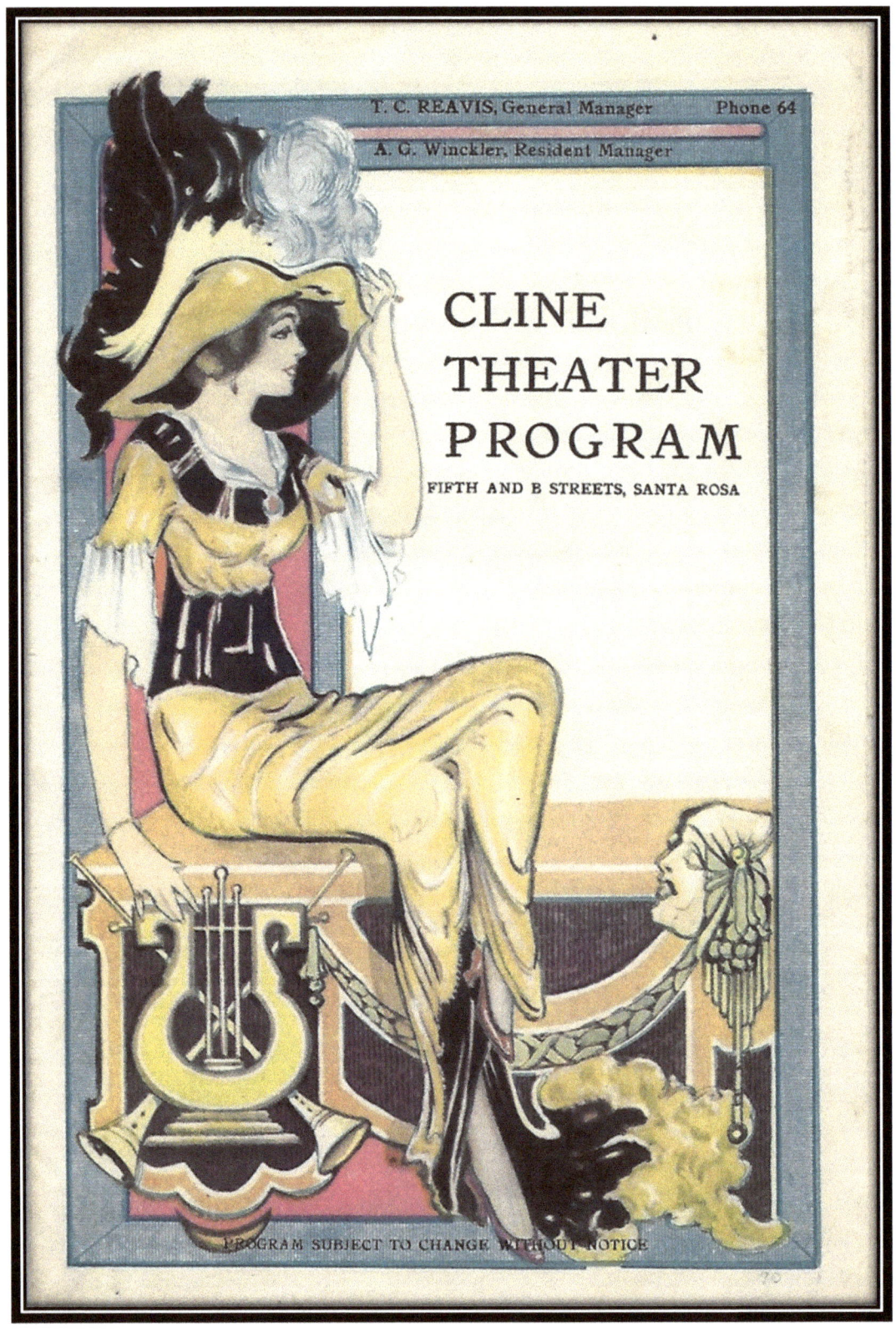

Fifth & B Streets Santa Rosa

Rose Theatre

SUNDAY, MARCH 12

WILLIAM RUSSELL
IN
"THE ROOF TREE"

Charles Hutchinson in—
Hurricane Hutch No. 8"

OTHER SHORT SUBJECTS

MATINEE, 2 to 5 — Adults, 15c. War tax
extra. Children, 10c. No war tax.

EVENING, 5 to 11 — Adults, 20c. War tax
extra. Children, 10c. No war tax.

MONDAY and TUESDAY
MARCH 13 and 14

AGNES AYERS
IN
"THE LANE THAT HAD NO TURNING"

Comedy—"Rolling Stones"

FOX NEWS

MATINEE, 2 to 5 — Adults, 15c. War tax
extra. Children, 10c. No war tax.

EVENING, 7 to 11 — Adults, 20c. War tax
extra. Children, 10c. No war tax.

WEDNESDAY, MARCH 15

BRYANT WASHBURN
IN
"THE ROAD TO LONDON"

Comedy—"Girls Will Be Girls"

Burton Holmes Travelogue

MATINEE, 2 to 5 — Adults, 15c. War tax
extra. Children, 10c. No war tax.

EVENING, 7 to 11 — Adults, 20c. War tax
extra. Children, 10c. No war tax.

THURSDAY and FRIDAY
MARCH 16 and 17

MARION DAVIES
IN
"THE BRIDES PLAY"

Comedy—"Squirrel Food"

INTERNATIONAL NEWS

MATINEE, 2 to 5 — Adults, 15c. War tax
extra. Children, 10c. No war tax.

EVENING, 7 to 11 — Adults, 20c. War tax
extra. Children, 10c. No war tax.

Marion Davies in the
Cosmopolitan Production
'The Brides Play'
A Paramount Picture

SATURDAY, MARCH 18

WINIFRED WESTOVER
IN
"ANN OF LITTLE SMOKEY"

SCENIC
By the Side of the Road

AESOP'S FABLES.

KINETO REVIEW

MATINEE, 2 to 5 — Adults, 15. War tax
extra. Children, 10c. No war tax.

EVENING, 7 to 11 — Adults, 20c. War tax
extra. Children, 10c. No war tax.

Rose Theater 1913-1944
638 Fourth Street
C. M. Carrington Proprietor

Cinema Treasurers Image
403 B Street

Will Call ticket purchased with Keegan Bros. advertisement.

The Elite Theater 1911 – 1929
518 Fourth Street
Mary A. McDannel Proprietor 1911 - 1929
C. N. Carrington Co-Owner 1911- 1912
Charles H. Ball Jr. Co-Owner 1912 -1929
Mrs. V. Langer owner 1929-1929

ROXY THEATER

Roxy corner of Fifth & B Street

Greyhound Bus Depot across from Roxy Theater

Cash Night at the Roxy Theater on Thursday's
Image Courtesy Cinema Treasures Collection

During the WWII years into the 1950's theaters had special promotions giving away cash, jewelry and dishes. Essentially a raffle, you deposited one side of the two-part ticket into a wire tumbler and tickets were drawn during intermission between movies. Yes, there were two movies, cartoons, news reels and on Saturdays a serial for kids.

Ticket was 15 cents, popcorn & a drink was "Two-Bits" (25 cents)

Tower Theater Night Scene
Fourth Street
Image Courtesy Cinema Treasures Collection

Entering the Tower Theater was a Classic Art Deco Hallway featuring 1930's
Scenes of a time past. Totally upscale with soft comfortable cushioned seating.

Interior featured large flowing curtains that would open up at the beginning of the first
movie. The walls were adorned with sconces and brilliant colors. The floor was carpeted
and an usher would lead you to your seating row by flashlight.

Cinema Treasurers image
Roxy on Santa Rosa Avenue

Tower Theater at 730 Fourth Street next to Library

California Theater
B Street next to Wolcott's Confectionary Stand

Image Courtesy Cinema Treasures Collection

Cash or Dish Night at the California Theater
Image Courtesy Cinema Treasures Collection

During the Depression and WWII movies were the entertainment of the day. No television, no cell phones, no personal Game Boys or computers. Most theaters featured cash, jewelry, dish or other give-away drawings during intermission to attract crowds. Seen here how successful give-away promotions were.

Notice the original marque on above photo changed in the 1950's.

Image Courtesy Cinema Treasures Collection

California Theater located on B Street next to Walcott's confectionary sweet shop who sold candy and popcorn prior to entering the theater. Once inside the theater a hot dog was .25 cents.

Inside the theater was also Art Deco with large ceiling lamps with multi colored glass facets and prisms.

The upstairs balcony was a teenage delight for various reasons; popcorn tossing to lower seating and as the teenager aged a "make-out" area.

BEST Pictures
Excellent Sound
Best Ventilation
Comfortable Seats

CALIFORNIA THEATRE
Phone 99   PETALUMA   Phone 99

ATTEND OUR MATINEES
General Admission, 25c
Loges, 35c

EVENING SHOWS 7:00 - 9:00 P. M.
Adults 35c   Students 25c   Kiddies 10c

MARCH, 1937

Matinee Daily at 2:00; Sunday 2:30
Adults 25c, Loges 35c (EXCEPT SUNDAY OR HOLIDAY)

SUNDAY	MONDAY	TUESDAY	WEDNESDAY	THURSDAY	FRIDAY	SATURDAY
Feb. 28	**Mar. 1**	**2**	**3**	**4**	**5**	**6**

Feb. 28 — Mar. 1

The Last Word in Entertainment . . . Set to Irving Berlin's Greatest Music . . . In a Show as Big as the Town . . . As Grand as the Melodies!

"On the Avenue"
WITH
DICK POWELL
Madeleine Carroll   Alice Faye
The Ritz Bros.

SPECIAL ATTRACTION WED.

2 — 3

Single Handed He Battled a New Kind of Public Enemy!

James Cagney
in His Greatest Role
"GREAT GUY"
with MAE CLARKE
— On the Same Bill —

YOU'LL LAFF OUT LOUD!
SING ME A LOVE SONG
with JAMES MELTON PATRICIA ELLIS

SPECIAL ATTRACTION WED.

4

THEY ONLY PAY THE BONUS ONCE!
LET'S MAKE A MILLION
EDW. EVERETT HORTON

ALSO
Mystery! Thrills! Romance!
"Sinner Take All"
WITH
BRUCE CABOT
MARGARET LINDSAY
JOSEPH CALLEIA

STAGE ATTRACTION FRIDAY

5 — 6

You Have Little Idea of What a HONEY OF A COMEDY THIS IS Until You See It!

Three SMART GIRLS
BINNIE BARNES   ALICE BRADY
NAN GREY   BARBARA READ

ALSO **GENERAL SPANKY**

7 — 8

ALLURING LOVELINESS THAT TAKES YOUR BREATH AWAY!

GOLD DIGGERS OF 1937
WITH
JOAN BLONDELL   DICK POWELL

SPECIAL ATTRACTION WED.

9 — 10

The Surging Glorious Romance of a Boy and Girl Who Fought a Mad World to Win Happiness!

Claudette COLBERT
Fred MacMURRAY
in Frank Lloyd's
"Maid of Salem"
ALSO

MURDER, MIRTH AND MATRIMONY!
SMART BLONDE
Glenda Farrell

SPECIAL ATTRACTION WED.

11 — 12

A Picture That Will Make Your Heart Pound With Tenseness! Thrill to the Most Glorious Romance Adventure of the Year!

MARLENE DIETRICH   CHARLES BOYER
The GARDEN OF ALLAH
In TECHNICOLOR

ALSO
"Follow Your Heart"
WITH
MICHAEL BARTLETT

STAGE ATTRACTION FRIDAY

13

Roughnecks and Romeos in a Hilarious Romance!
Victor McLAGLEN
Preston Foster
Ida Lupino
IN
"Sea Devils"
ALSO
'Captain's Kid'
WITH
SYBIL JASON
GUY KIBBEE
MAY ROBSON

14 — 15

It's Bigger . . . Faster . . . Funnier Than "Libeled Lady"!

Joan CRAWFORD
William POWELL
Robert MONTGOMERY
Frank MORGAN
IN
'The Last of Mrs. Cheyney'

SPECIAL ATTRACTION WED.

16 — 17

ONE FLIRTATIOUS HOUR BLASTED TWENTY-FIVE YEARS OF BLISS!
New laurels for the book and the play!
DODSWORTH
WALTER HUSTON
RUTH CHATTERTON
MARY ASTOR
PAUL LUKAS
Selected Short Subjects

SPECIAL ATTRACTION WED.

18 — 19

THE FAMOUS NOVEL...NOW ON THE SCREEN!
"Anthony Adverse"
with FREDRIC MARCH
OLIVIA De HAVILLAND
ANITA LOUISE   CLAUDE RAINS
A Warner Bros.-First National Picture

20

The Law Against the Lawless in the Thrill Story of All Seasons!
PAT O'BRIEN
Humphrey Bogart
IN
"The Great O'Malley"
Stage Attraction

21 — 22

You'll Meet a New and Different Grace Moore . . . Completely Madcap in Her Gayest and Liveliest Romance!

GRACE MOORE
IN
"When You're in Love"
WITH
CARY GRANT

SPECIAL ATTRACTION WED.

23 — 24

Their Love Affair Was a Notorious Scandal!
"STOLEN HOLIDAY"
Kay Francis
with IAN HUNTER
ALSO

THRILL TO GAY, GLORIOUS SONG
Nino MARTINI
"THE GAY DESPERADO"
with LEO CARRILLO IDA LUPINO

SPECIAL ATTRACTION WED.

25

HILARIOUS!
CHARLIE JOINS THE BOY SCOUTS!
CHARLIE RUGGLES
ALICE BRADY
MIND YOUR OWN BUSINESS
WITH
LYLE TALBOT
BENNY BAKER
ALSO
"Fugitive in the Sky"

STAGE ATTRACTION FRIDAY

26 — 27

Here's the Picture You're Waiting For . . .
EDNA FERBER'S MASTERPIECE
TIMBERLAND DRAMA!
COME and GET IT
with *Edward Arnold*
FRANCES FARMER   JOEL McCREA
— On the Same Bill —
"BULLDOG DRUMMOND ESCAPES" with RAY MILLAND
A PARAMOUNT PICTURE

TRANSPORTATION
FRED WISEMAN AVIATOR – U. S. MAIL DELIVERY

Early aviator who is credited delivering the first U.S. Air Mail which was from Petaluma to Santa Rosa. He crash-landed in Cotati & repaired the Air Ship and continued to Santa Rosa. Wiseman built his own plane competing in U.S. flying competitions.

AVIATOR WISEMAN AND OFFICIALS ATTACHING A BAROGRAPH IMMEDIATELY BEFORE THE ENDURANCE RECORD TRIAL.

FRED. J. WISEMAN
AVIATOR
SANTA ROSA, CAL.

WISEMAN FLYING 48 MILES PER HOUR OVER THE SCORE BOARD, SELFRIDGE FIELD

FRED. J. WISEMAN
AVIATOR
SANTA ROSA, CAL.

Wiseman's Air Ship was purchased, restored by the Smithsonian and now hangs on display in the Washington D.C. United States Postal Service building.

PETALUMA & SANTA ROSA RAILROAD CARS

Building shown on card is still standing housing Chevy's Mexican Restaurant across from Railroad Square on Fourth & Wilson Streets.

Employees Badge Petaluma & Santa Rosa Railway Company

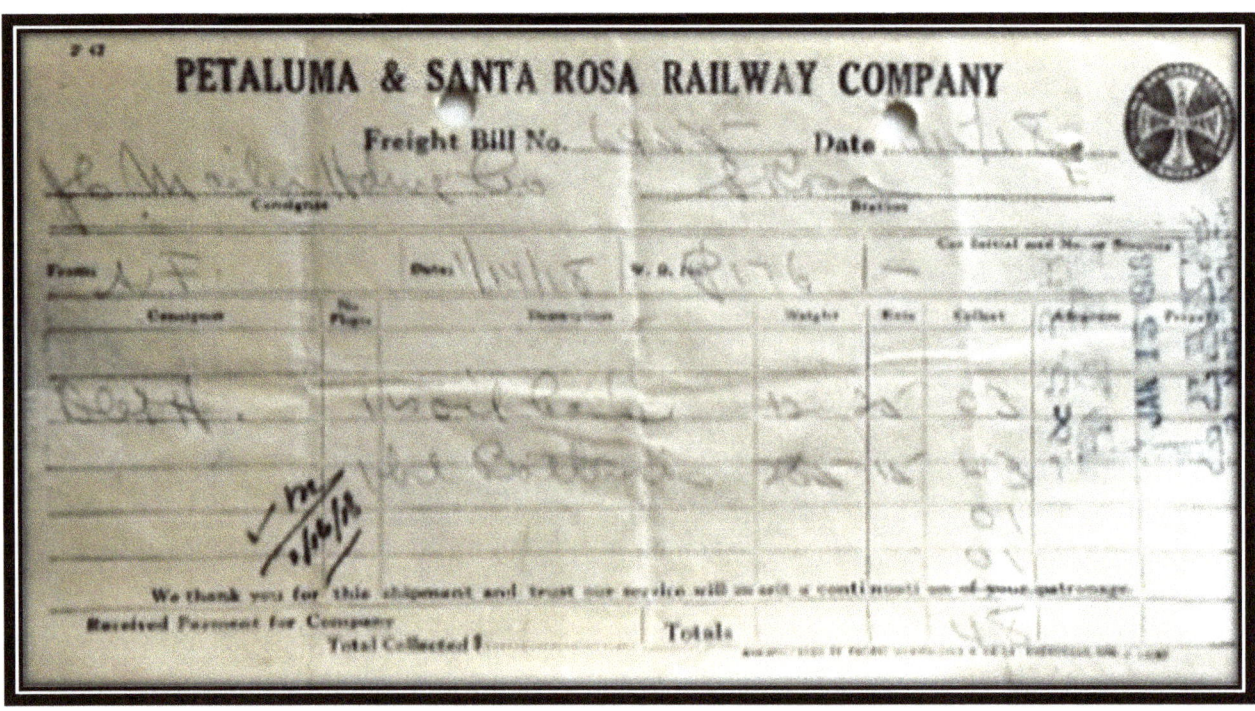

Petaluma & Santa Rosa Railway Bill of Lading

Petaluma and Santa Rosa
Railroad Company

OPERATES

OVERNIGHT
FREIGHT SERVICE

BETWEEN

ALL POINTS

SUPPORT YOUR RAILROAD

Advertisement

Advertisement

Additional Advertisements
Front & back of the same card

Ink blotters were also a form of advertisement as they were always sitting in full view on a person's desk. Colorful advertisement always brough one's eyes to the cards.

Top card states door to door delivery. Bottom card features the building housing Chevy's Mexican Restaurant advertising door to door service to Santa Rosa, Sebastopol and Petaluma.

CALIFORNIA NORTHWESTERN R. R. DEPOT. SANTA ROSA, CAL.

Both images feature Railroad Depot at Fourth & Wilson Streets

North Western Pacific Depot, Santa Rosa, Cal.

2207

Northwestern Pacific Railroad Depot at Railroad Square Lower Fourth Street

Southern Pacific Railroad Depot on North Street

EARLY STREET CARS

Horse drawn trolley in front of Western Hotel near train depot on lower Fourth St

Horse drawn trolley with passengers. Appears this is the boarding station for the trolley.

Electric trolley in front of Santa Rosa Library

Electric trolley car on upper Fourth Street near McDonald Avenue

Horse & buggy in front of Soda Works & Barber Shop

Vacationers sightseeing on way to Mark West Springs, seen in background

STAGECOACH BY MONTGOMERY WARDS

Montgomery Wards & Redwood Rose Stage Depot on Mendocino Avenue

Redwood Rose Stagecoach next to Montgomery Wards

WM. H. HUDSON SODA WORKS

NELLIGAN & SON FEED STORE

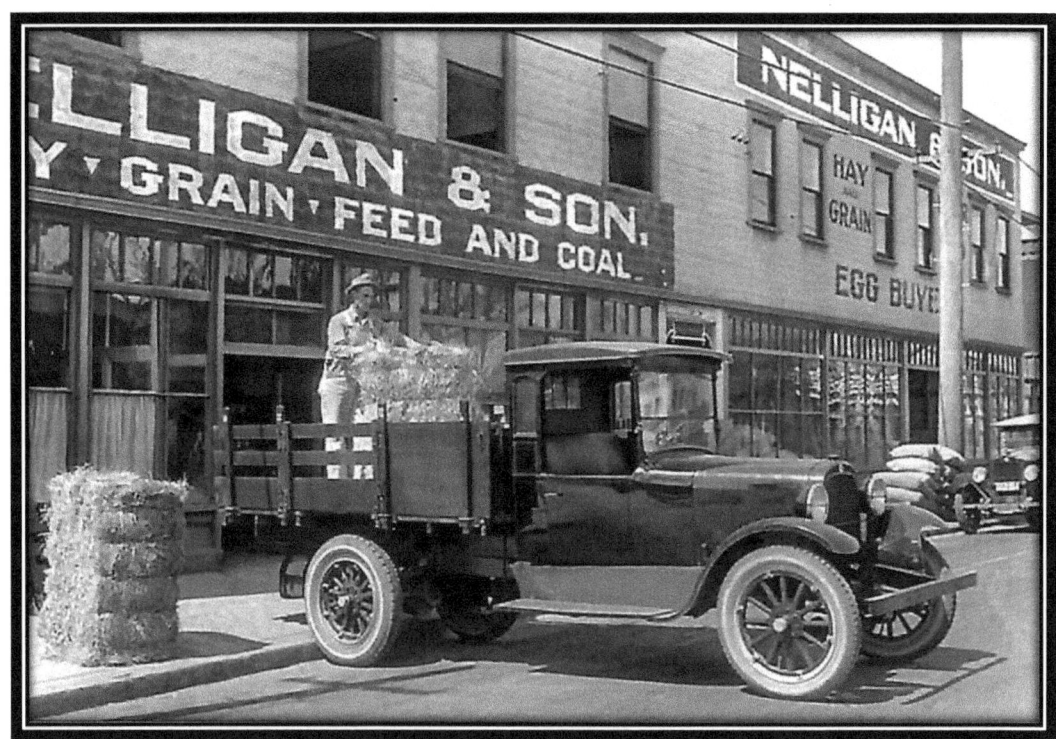

Lee Bros. Moving Van, C. 1918

Oldfield tire advertisement featuring Barney Oldfield's race car numbered 999

LUTHER BURBANK

Greenhouse next to Burbank's house on Santa Rosa Avenue
Experimental room

Corners Santa Rosa Avenue & Tupper Street
View of Luther Burbank Santa Rosa Experiment Grounds

Showing Burbank's new house on left and row of houses on Tupper Street
Looking northeast

LUTHER BURBANK SALESMAN SEED BOX

Stocks
Dwarf 10 Weeks Mixed
(Standard Variety)
10c.

THE LUTHER BURBANK CO.
Sole Distributer of the Burbank Horticultural Productions
SAN FRANCISCO, CALIFORNIA, U. S. A.

Burbank Fragrance Verbena
Extra Select
25c.

THE LUTHER BURBANK CO.
Sole Distributer of the Burbank Horticultural Productions
SAN FRANCISCO, CALIFORNIA, U. S. A.

Crimson Morning Glory
Burbank Giant
10c.

THE LUTHER BURBANK CO.
Sole Distributer of the Burbank Horticultural Productions
SAN FRANCISCO, CALIFORNIA

Dianthus Imperialis Mixed
Burbank
10c.

THE LUTHER BURBANK CO.
Sole Distributer of the Burbank Horticultural Production

SPINELESS CACTUS DEVELOPED FOR CATTLE FORAGE AND FRUIT CUTTINGS

PRICE LIST AND ORDER BLANK

Burbank's Spineless Cactus
The Luther Burbank Company
Exposition Building, Pine and Battery Sts.
SAN FRANCISCO, CALIFORNIA

FOR FORAGE CUTTINGS				FOR FRUIT CUTTINGS			
	Each	Ten	100	1000		Each	Ten	100
					Quillota (Yellow Fruit)	$2	$15	$100
Selected Forage Cactus .60	$5	$40	$300	Niagara (Crimson Fruit) $1.50	$12	$75

Please ship via...the following cactus cuttings:

State whether express or freight

Ship...

State when to ship

FOR FORAGE

Number of Cuttings		Price
	Selected Forage Cactus $ ....

FOR FRUIT

	Quillota	$ ....
	Niagara	$ ....

Enclosed find ....

State whether check, draft or money order

for $ .... in payment of the above order

Write plainly.   Name ....

Shipping Address...(Town)

....(County)

Date ....191.....   (State)

If shipping destination and Post Office are different, give Post Office Address below.

NONE GENUINE WITHOUT SEAL

TRADE MARK
THIS SEAL GUARANTEES A GENUINE LUTHER BURBANK PRODUCTION

All plants and cuttings lightly and carefully packed with *No charges for boxes or packing. Freight or express charges to be paid by purchaser. No cuttings sent by mail.*
All orders must be accompanied by the purchase price.
The right is reserved to reject any order.
See last page of Catalogue for shipping information.
Orders for delivery before July 1st, 1913, will be accepted, if accompanied by a cash deposit of 25 per cent of the total purchase price.

Luther Burbank and his wonderful thornless Cactus, Santa Rosa, Cal.

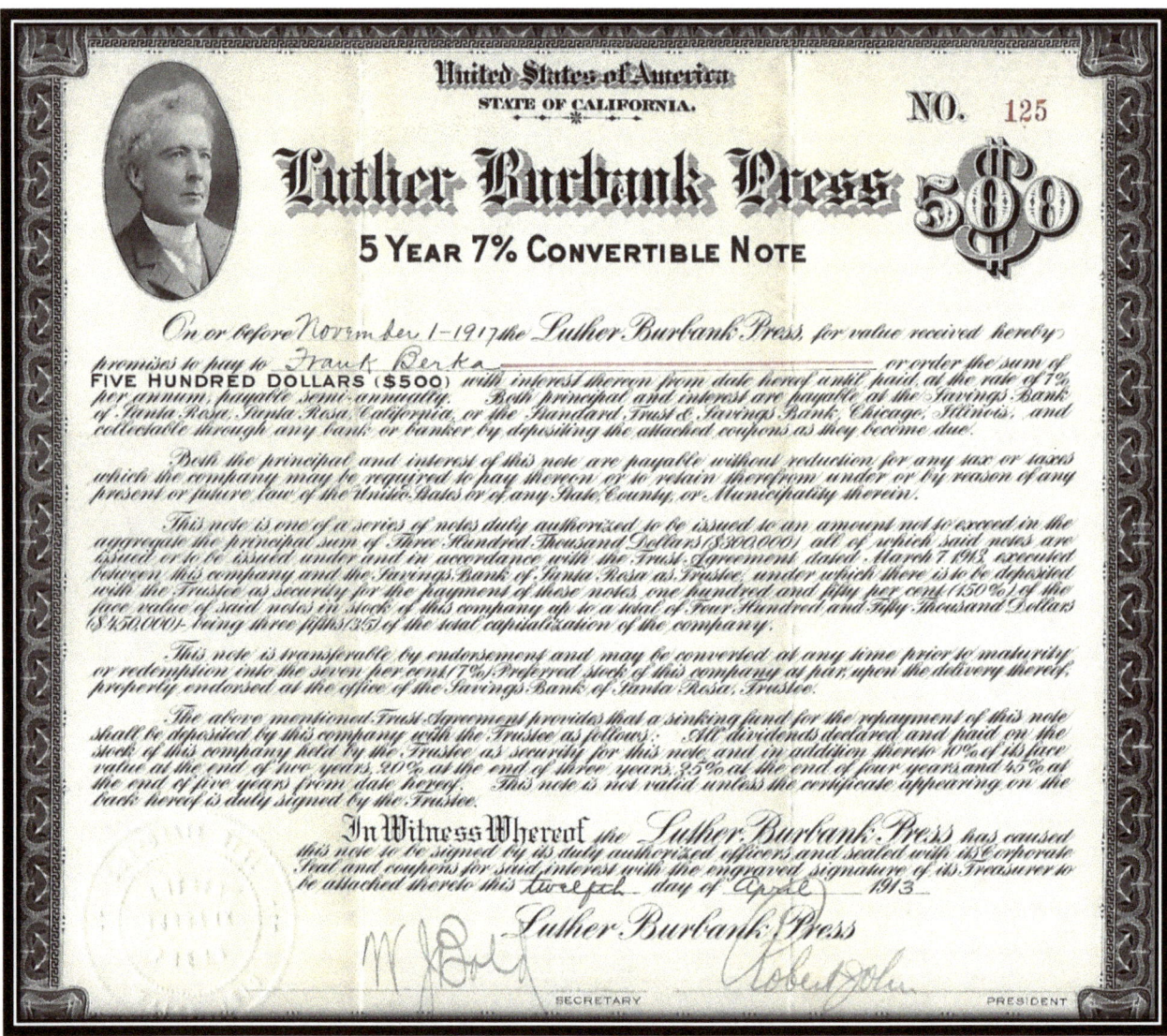

PRINCIPAL PAYABLE ON OR BEFORE NOVEMBER 1, 1917
AT SAVINGS BANK OF SANTA ROSA
OR
STANDARD TRUST & SAVINGS BANK CHICAGO, ILL.

QUEEN GERALDINE *Grace*
SANTA ROSA JUVENILE CARNIVAL
MAY 18, 1907

Queen Geraldine
Juvenile Rose Carnival
Santa Rosa, Cal. May 18, 1907

Santa Rosa Junior Carnival 1907
Queen Geraldine Grace

Great Rose Carnival 1912
Juvenile Queen Ester June

Queen's Carnival Float 1908

1908 Queen Nancy's Celebration

May McMeans 1911 Adult Queen

Lucille Fulwider 1911 Juvenile Queen

X. Y. C. Members on Float 1909

1910 X. Y. C. Club Natural Flower Float

Clarence Thompson Natural Flower Float 1910

Patriotic WWI Float May 1919

Downtown parade route around Santa Rosa Court House Square

Mayor See's Auto

Ladies preparing for parade in both photos May 1913

Group photo of participants in parade

Parade team marching along with parade

Asian participants May 1917 Rose Carnival

Native Sons Golden West Santa Rosa Chapter 28

1912 Parade scene with J. C. Mailer Hardware on right side

Hadrich & Company seen in background 1912

Christian Bible School Float C.1915

U.S. Navy Blue Jackets in Parade 1908

U. S. Navy Blue Jackets Marching Band in Parade 1911

Street scene on Fourth Street

Digintarys with Luther Burbank third row right rear seat May 13, 1917

Grand Army of the Republic c. 1910-1912

Fourth Street Court House Square c. 1912

All three photos 1908 at showing the end of the parade

Burbank Souvenir Golden Jubilee Program May 1923

Santa Rosa native Sons Building Main Street (Mendocino Avenue) C. 1910

Native Sons Ribbons dating 1897, 1909 & 1911

TELEPHONE COMPANY

Santa Rosa telephone Staff c.1922

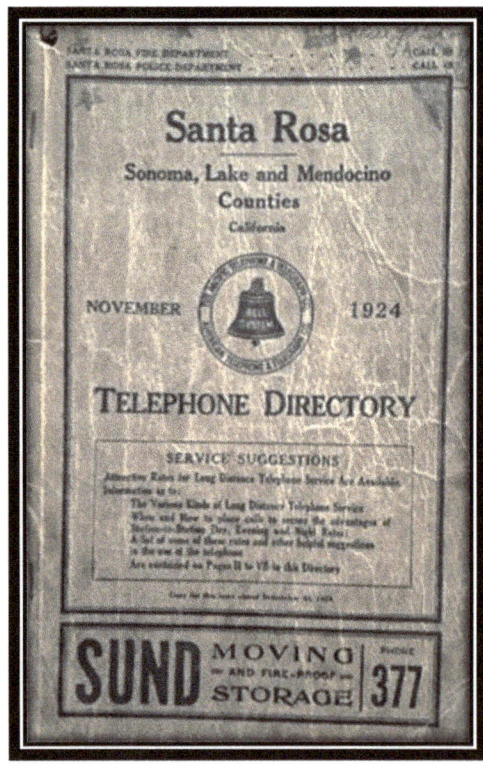

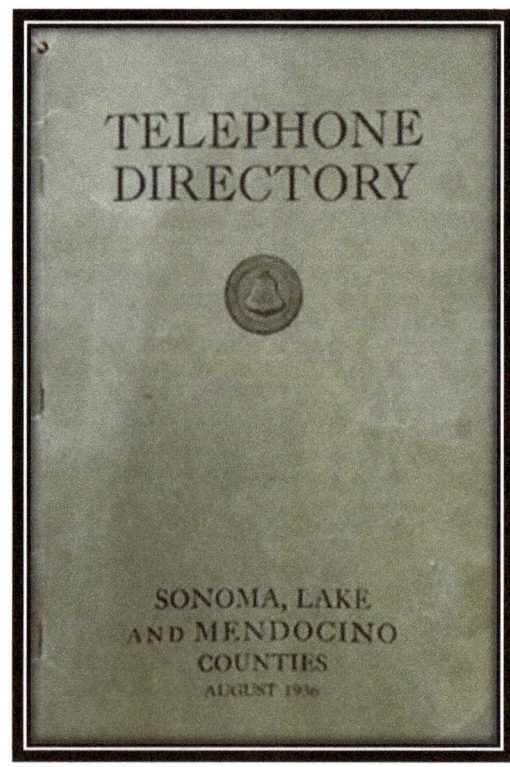

Yes, May I Help You. C. 1907

POST OFFICE

U.S. Post Office Santa Rosa postcard dated September 1912

U. S. Post Office c. 1940s now Sonoma County Museum

HARDISTY'S

4th St. Santa Rosa 1924

Hardisty's on right side of card Occidental Hotel on left side

THE WHITE HOUSE

White House eastside corner 4th & B Streets

ROSENBERG'S

Rosenberg's Department Store southeast corner 4th & D Street

STAGE DEPOT

Redwood Rose Motor Stage
Redwood Highway North now Mendocino Avenue

Redwood Rose Auto Center
Redwood Highway North now Mendocino Avenue

Entrance to Redwood Rose Auto Center
Redwood Highway North now Mendocino Avenue

Ford Sales Agent at 808 Tupper Street

FORD AGENCY

Ford Agency Authorized Sales & Service Main Street
(Now Mendocino Avenue)

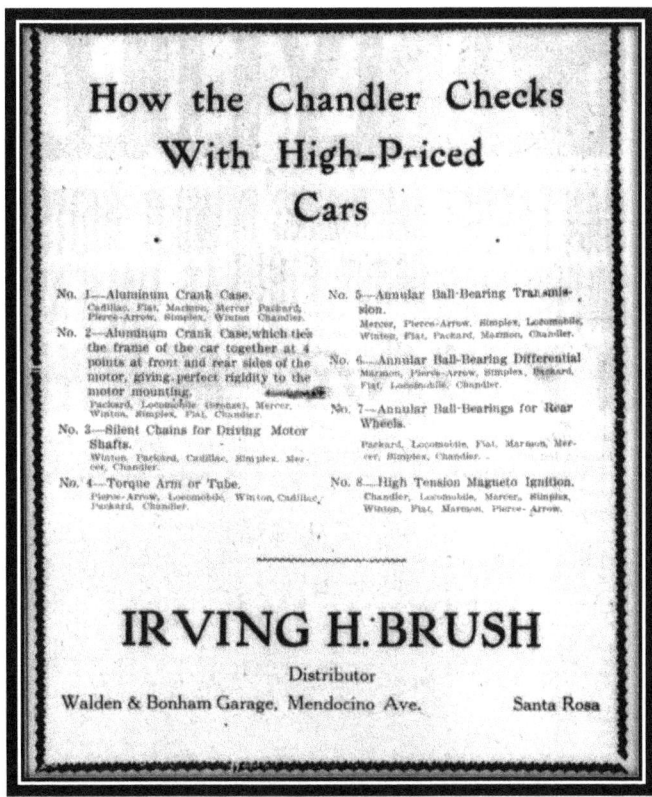

Chandler Four Door Sedan late 1920s
Walden & Bonham Garage
Mendocino Avenue

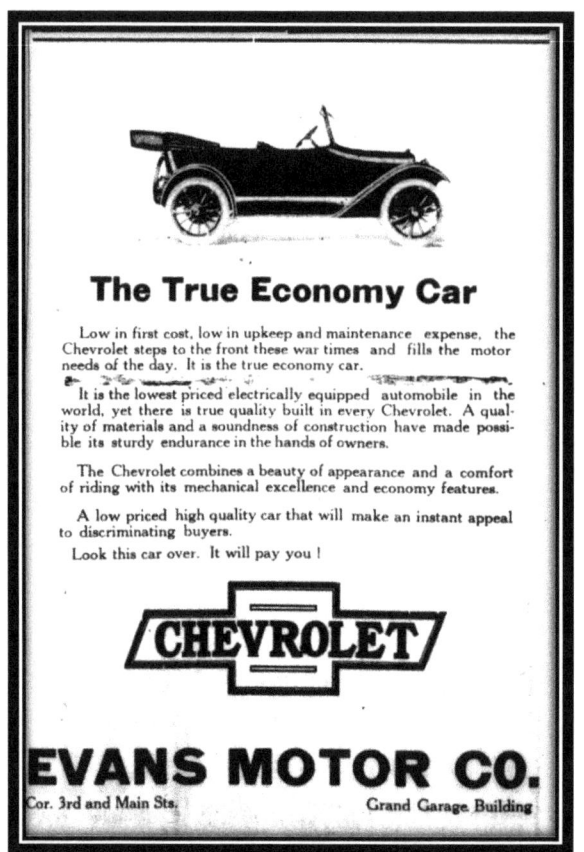

The True Economy Car

Low in first cost, low in upkeep and maintenance expense, the Chevrolet steps to the front these war times and fills the motor needs of the day. It is the true economy car.

It is the lowest priced electrically equipped automobile in the world, yet there is true quality built in every Chevrolet. A quality of materials and a soundness of construction have made possible its sturdy endurance in the hands of owners.

The Chevrolet combines a beauty of appearance and a comfort of riding with its mechanical excellence and economy features.

A low priced high quality car that will make an instant appeal to discriminating buyers.

Look this car over. It will pay you !

CHEVROLET

EVANS MOTOR CO.

Cor. 3rd and Main Sts.   Grand Garage Building

Evans Chevrolet Motor Co.
Corner Third & Main Street

C. M. WOLCOTT

F. A. YOUNG

WOLCOTT & YOUNG
Auto Laundry & Storage
Cars Washed Day or Night

Fifth Street Between Post
Office and Cline Theater

SANTA ROSA, CAL.

(OVER)

Table of Distances from Santa Rosa

Agua Caliente...18	Geyserville 24	Penngrove 10
Bellevue 4	Glen Ellen......15	Petaluma 16
Bloomfield 14	Guerneville 20	Petrified Forest.14
Bodega 17	Healdsburg 16	Pine Flat 22
Burke's 5	Hopland ......,44	Sebastopol 7
Cotati ...., 9	Kellogg 16	Schellville 25
Calistoga 20	Kenwood 12	Skaggs Springs..30
Camp Meeker...15	Lakeport 75	Sonoma 22
Cazadero 30	Lakeville 20	St. Helena......20
Cloverdale 34	Lytton 20	Stony Point....12
Duncans 27	Mark West Spg. 9	Tomales 20
El Verano......20	Melitta 5	Trenton 12
Forestville 12	Mirabel Park....14	Valley Ford 18
Freestone 13	Mt. Olivet 8	Ukiah 60
Fulton 5	Napa 34	Windsor 10
Geysers 45	Occidental 14	Yountville 29

Business Card showing mileage table

Grace Bros Brewery & Ice Plant 1897 image

NATIONAL ICE & COLD STORAGE

Off Sebastopol Avenue

Home Ice Delivery Request Sign

A. Giovannini Advertisement
Early Fox illustration

Santa Rosa Flour Mill
Wilson Street near train tracks

NELLIGAN & SON GRAIN, FEED & COAL
2nd & B Streets

GODFREY HARNESS & SADDLERY
Third Street

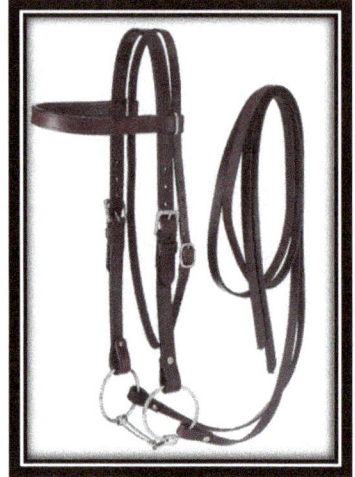

H. E. MEDLEY
Cyclist in front of H. E. Medley Piano tuning & repair shop.
120 Fifth Street

CARNATION CHAMPION

A Carnation a Day Keeps the Blues Away

1876

World's
Record
24,090
Carnations
In 66
Years

Confidence
In
Him
Means
Success
For You

1943

WALTER F. PRICE

A Pioneer in the Real Estate and Insurance Profession

215 B Street   **REALTOR**   **Phone 566**

Santa Rosa, California

(Over)

Santa Rosa, Sonoma County, California, the home of Ex-Senator Walter F. Price, whose record for the past 66 years places him as the world's champion in wearing a red carnation in the button hole of his coat, a total of 24,090. Here the carnations grow the year around.

Santa Rosa, the capitol of Sonoma County—the 8th county in the United States in agricultural production. Everything that grows anywhere grows everywhere in Sonoma County. Small farms and prosperous farmers. Railroad, waterways and fine highways. Bodega Bay. 3 large air ports. Rivers and Redwood forests—ocean beaches—fishing and hunting a plenty. Mountains and valleys—petrified forests—the geysers—Spanish missions. Russian Fort—the Valley of the Moon—some moonshine but mostly sunshine. On the wonderful Redwood highway, along the Pacific coast, the most beautiful drive in the world. The Garden of Eden—the Italy of the West—beautiful homes, churches and colleges. Large church built from one Redwood tree. The women most beautiful and the men robust. The land of fruits and flowers, all of it, make it a paradise on earth—out here in California where it is a pleasure just to live. Locate yourself and be contented. Believe it or not.

Noonan Meat Packing Plant after 1906 Earthquake

Campbell & Coffey Monuments
29 South Main Street near bridge (Now Santa Rosa Avenue)

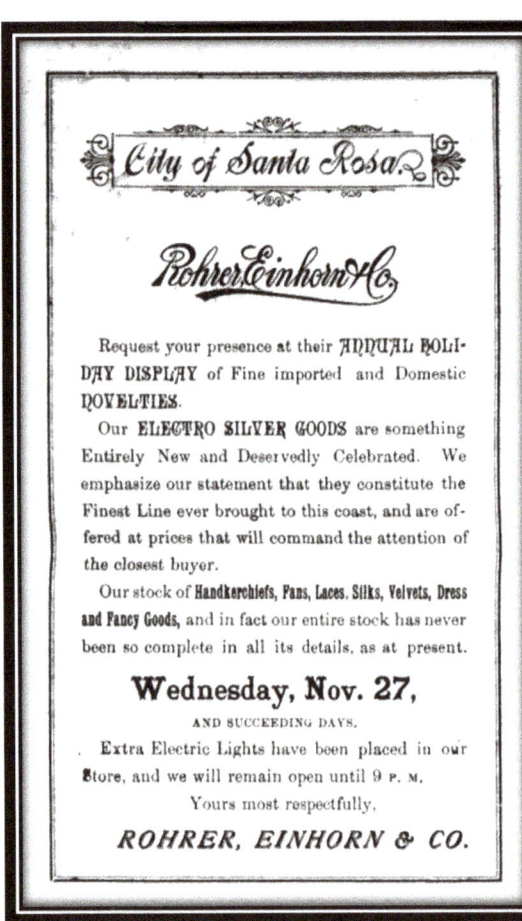

Rohrer Einhorn & Co. Department Store Fourth & B Street prior to White House

Feliziana Beniacasa At Train Depot 1919
Santa Rosa Creamery
Velvet Ice Cream owned by Grace Bros. 2ⁿᵈ & Davis Streets

 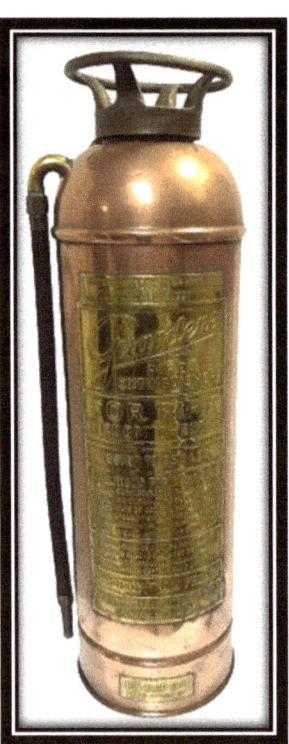 

Two Red Fire Extinguisher bombs on each side of Copper Extinguisher

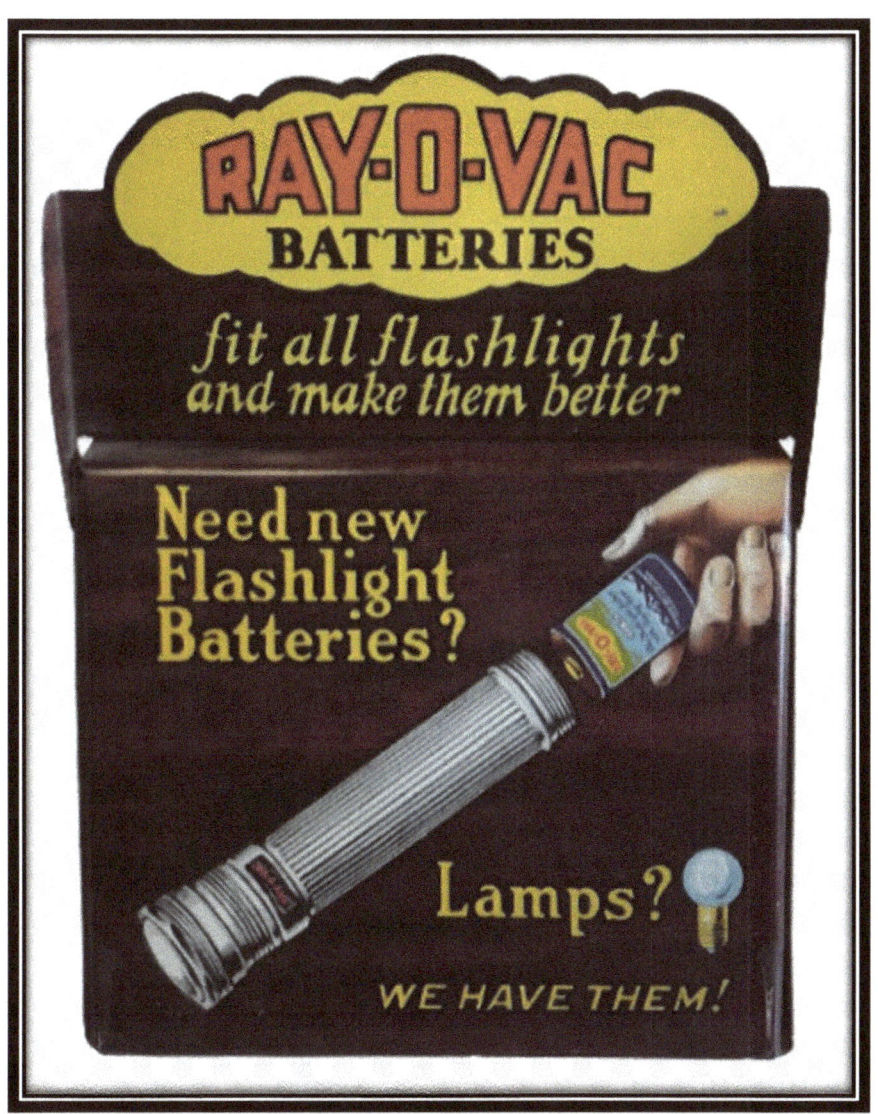

Sales display, battery & light bulb tester

Hardware & Sporting store display

Speer bullet identification board

Toilet Paper Holder

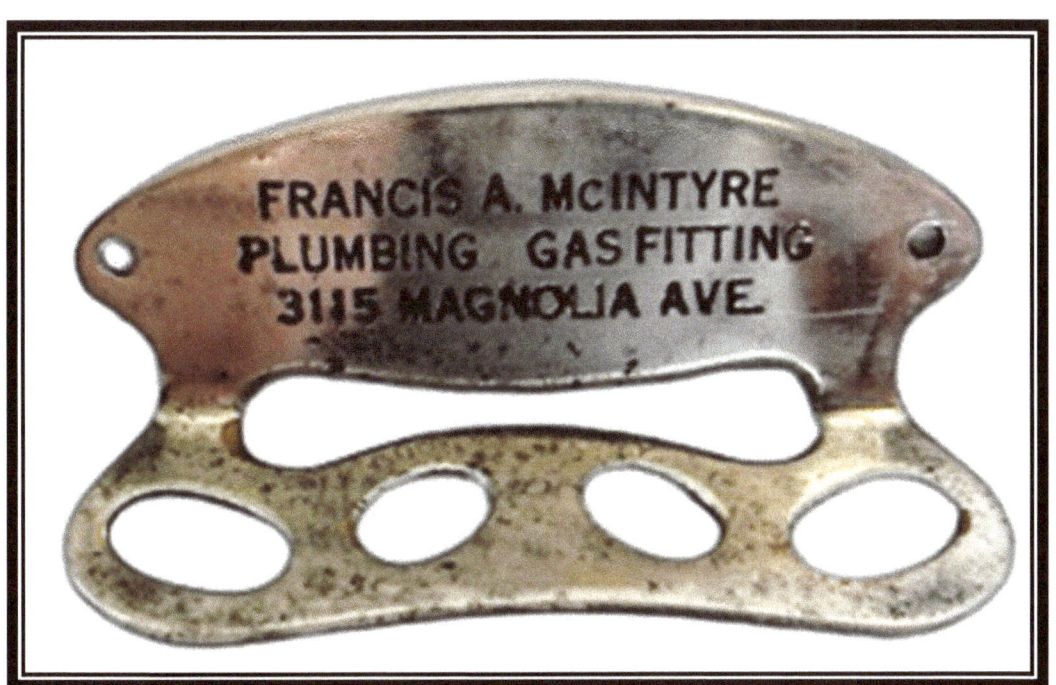

Toothbrush Holder

Mailer – Frey Hardware Store Bag

Dixon Hardware Notebook

Ketterlin Bros Hardware Notebook

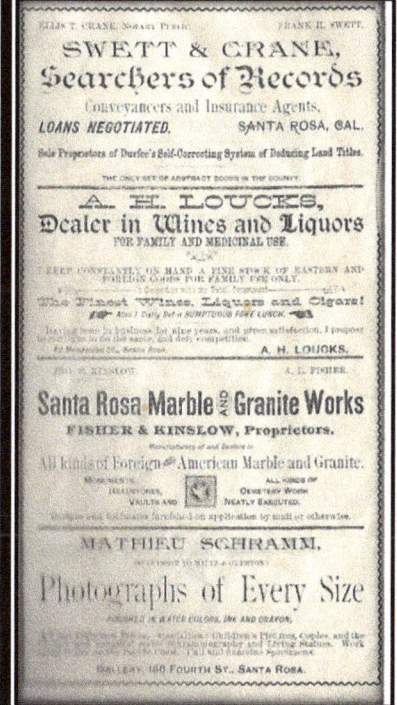

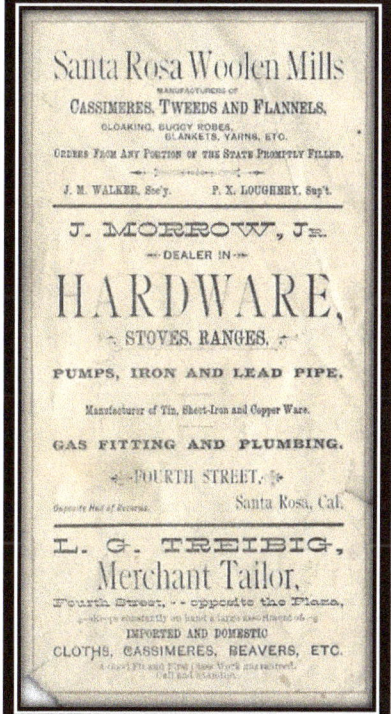

Geo. C. Jones
Book & Job printer
Santa Rosa, Cal.

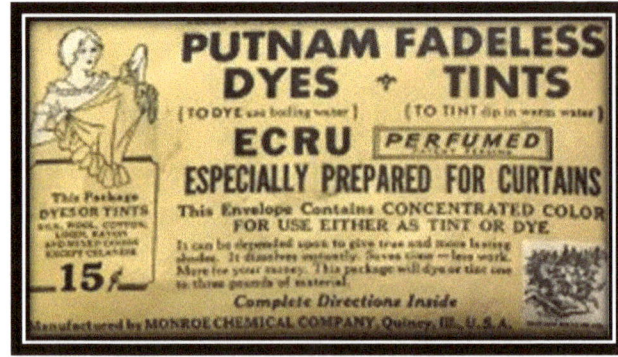

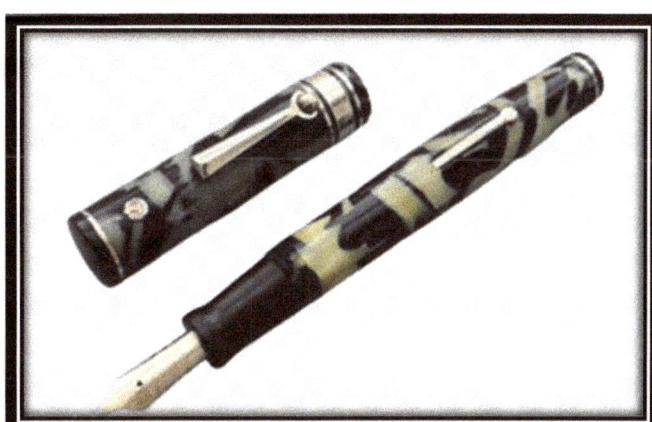

Wahl –Eversharp Lighted Window Display

J. H. Hunt, Santa Rosa, Cal.

Rose City Canning Co

California Fruit Canners Association

Santa Rosa Packing Co.

Cutting Packing Co.

Front of pocket mirror advertisement

Hunt Brothers Fruit Packing Plant

PRINDLE & KURLANDER

Wholesale Dealers in

CIGARS, TOBACCO, CIGARETTES PIPES, CHOCOLATES, GUMS, ETC.

225 Fourth Street   Phone 441 J
Santa Rosa, California

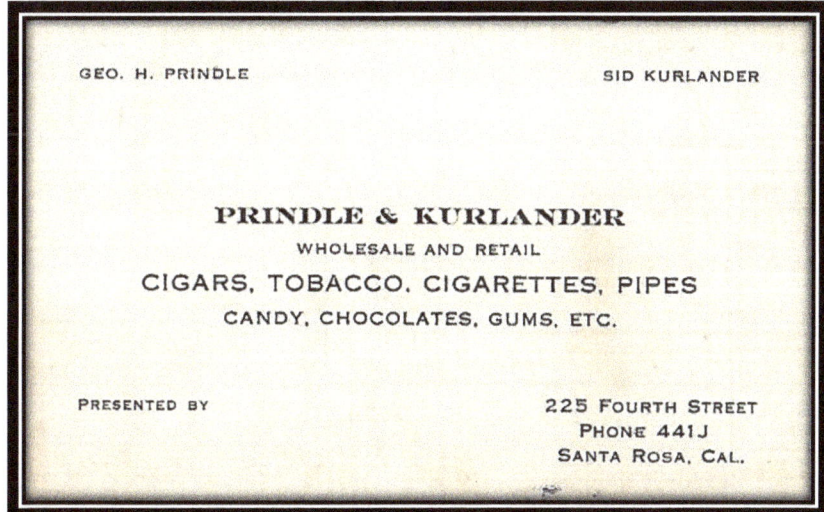

GEO. H. PRINDLE   SID KURLANDER

PRINDLE & KURLANDER
WHOLESALE AND RETAIL
CIGARS, TOBACCO, CIGARETTES, PIPES
CANDY, CHOCOLATES, GUMS, ETC.

PRESENTED BY   225 FOURTH STREET
PHONE 441J
SANTA ROSA, CAL.

CIGAR STORE TRADE TOKENS

TOKENS FROM MERLE AVILA COLLECTION

CIGAR STORES

Interior John David Hinshaw's Cigar Store c. 1920

Cigar Cutter
Used to nip off the end of a cigar before lighting.

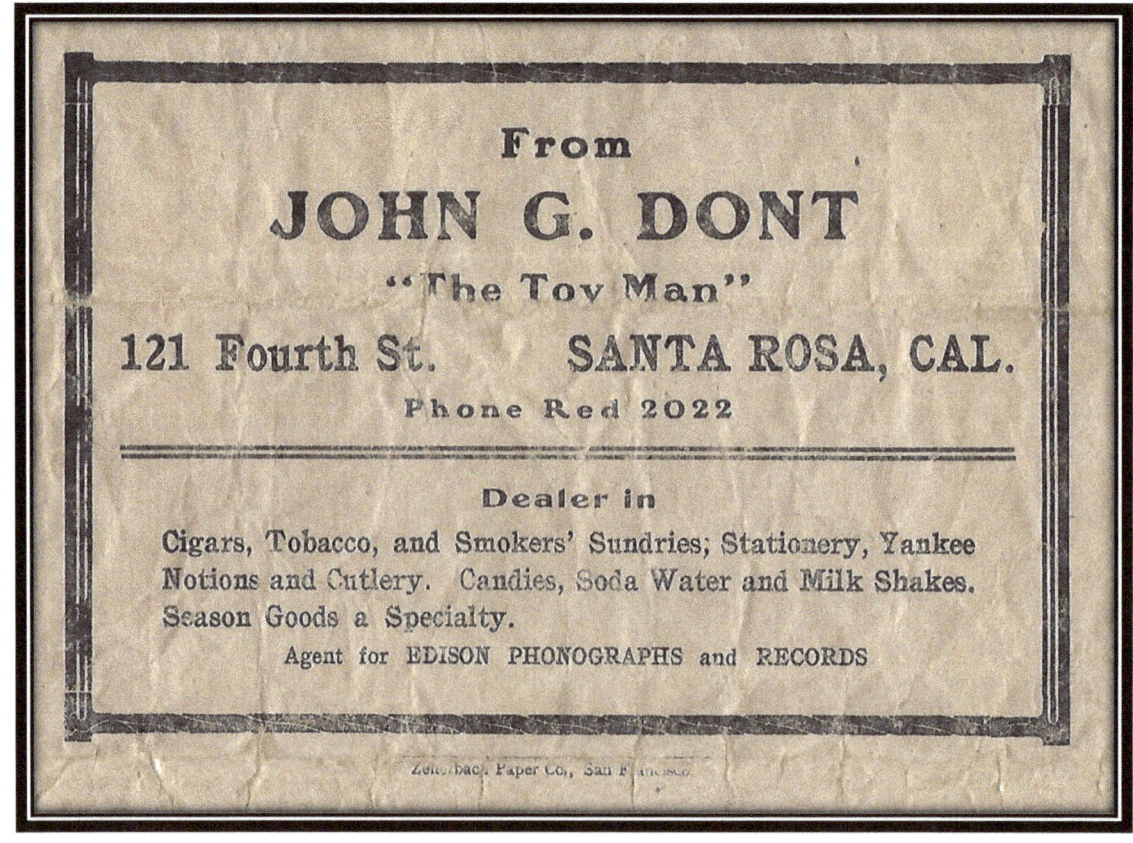

From
JOHN G. DONT

"The Toy Man"

121 Fourth St.   SANTA ROSA, CAL.

Phone Red 2022

Dealer in

Cigars, Tobacco, and Smokers' Sundries; Stationery, Yankee Notions and Cutlery. Candies, Soda Water and Milk Shakes. Season Goods a Specialty.

Agent for EDISON PHONOGRAPHS and RECORDS

Kurlander Advertisement
Dennis Kurlander Collection

Front & Back Kurlander Watch Fob

ADVERTISEMENTS

ADVERTISEMENTS

1936 Twilight Baseball League

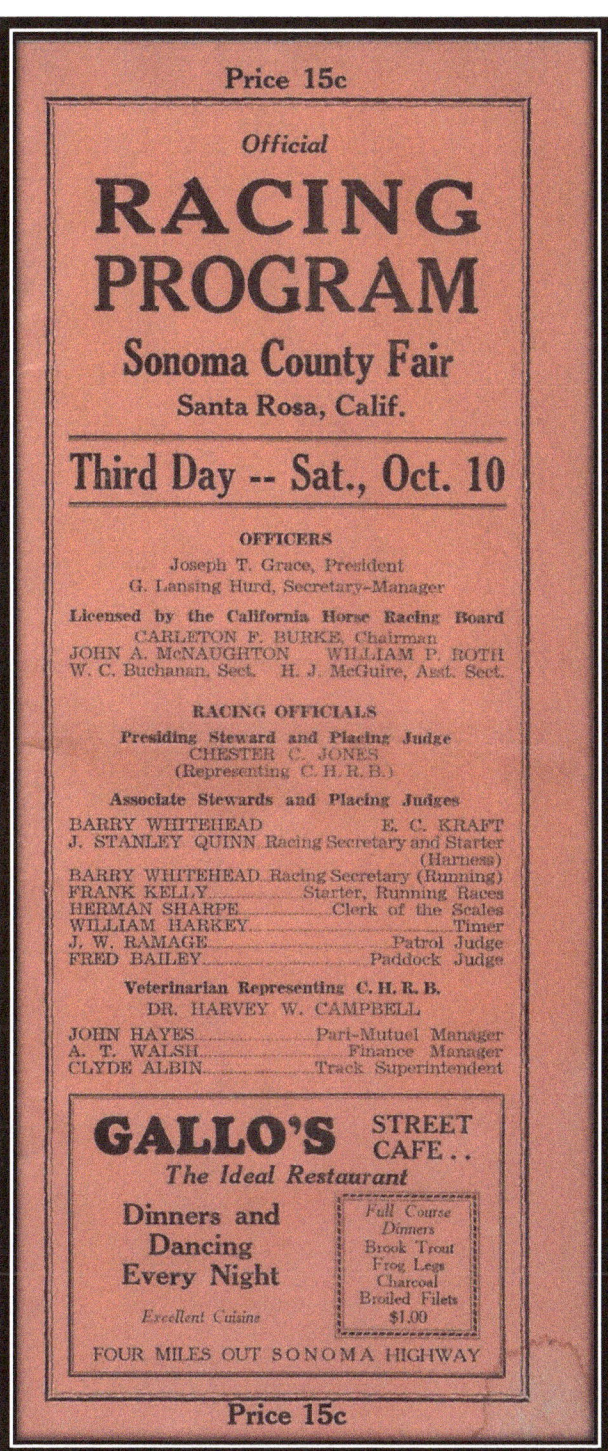

Horse Racing
Sonoma County Fair

Top row, left to right: H. C. Skow, Manager; H. Green, 1b; J. Prolo, 2b; H. Blennerhassett, lf; W. Simas, rf; N. Strader, c; J. O'Rourke, scorekeeper. *Bottom row, left to right:* F. Muzzi, utility; C. Hardt, p; W. Gonsales, ss; Frankie Banducci, bat boy; A. McCoy, cf., and G. Fitzgerald, utility.

Back Row: Gerald Mandish, Al L. Emeldi, H. Blennerhassett, Harry Skow, Manager; Carl Escobar, Norman "Red" Strader, Dick Powers. *Front Row:* Elmer Corbett, Billy Gonsales, Pat Clifford, Mario Bussa, Dave McNeil, Frank Banducci, Mascot.

Grace Bros. Baseball Team
Photos Oakland Tribune 1940

Santa Rosa Rose Buds c. 1927

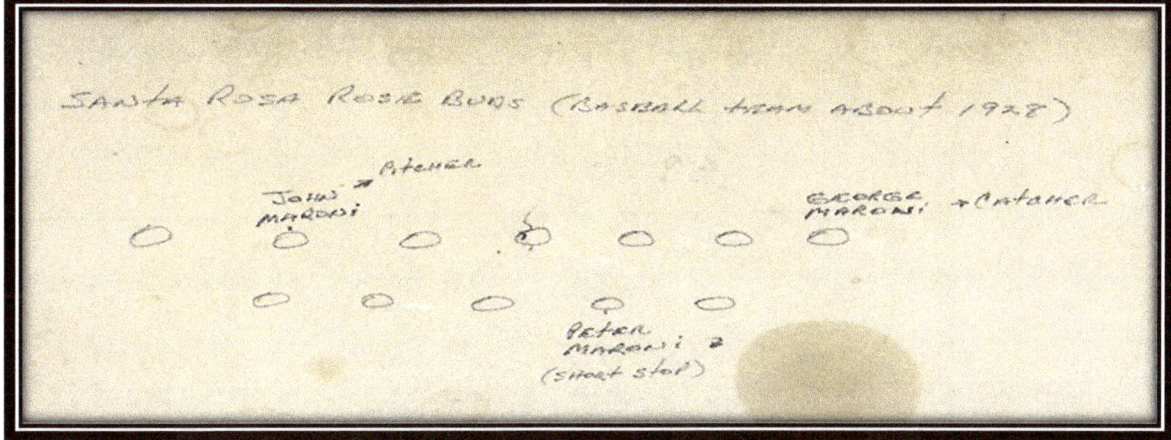

NEW ICE RINK OPENS TONIGHT

The Redwood Empire's newest center, the Sonoma County Ice Palace, will be formally opened tonight with a brilliant spectacle featuring outstanding ice skaters of the state and nation.

The ice rink, located at the corner of Second Street and Railroad Avenue, just west of the Grace Brothers plant, will be the mecca for thousands from Sonoma and neighboring counties.

Advanced sale of seats, in progress here for the past week, indicating a "sell-out" for the opening performance, this will be followed by public skating.

Freezing of the ice floor was started yesterday, and by opening time tonight, a two-inch surface of glass-smooth ice will be provided.

Mayor Robert Madison will make the opening address following introduction of Joseph T. Grace of the Grace Brothers Company. Already many local parties have reserved skates for the frolic which will follow the colorful revue.

Instructors will be on duty at all times to teach ice-skating to men, women and children. Every possible feature for convenience of the skating public and spectators is being provided in the huge Ice Palace, first of its kind in Northern California.

AMONG STARS HERE TONIGHT

Santa Rosa High School 1935 Football Awards

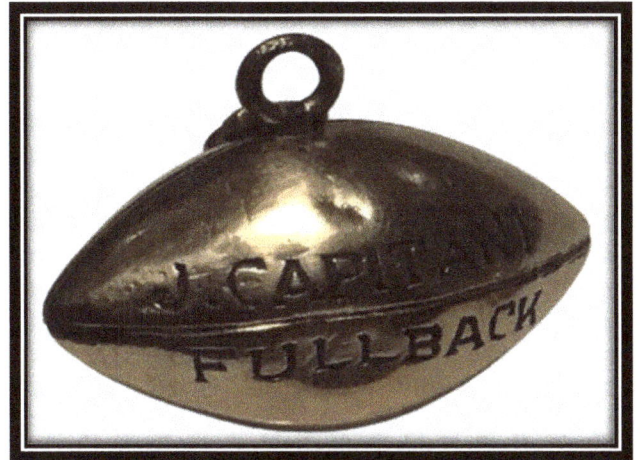

1892 Santa Rosa High School Football Team

1935 Santa Rosa High School Football Team at practice

Front Row> Norman Capitani,Ken Chaven,Howard Wells,Unknown,
Saunders,Ross Hamlin,Lee Weathington
Back Row> Unknown,Ed Green,Harold Kenney,Ralph Gambogi

1935 & 1936 Santa Rosa High School Football Teams

Top row (left to right): Beals, Lombardi, Barbieri, H. Kinnie, Maxwell, W. Kinnie, Alkire, Ridolfi, Doyle, Smith, Lafranconi, Bohan, Zumwalt. *Third row:* Freedom, Armstrong, Lange, Butler, Dittmer, Farrais, Miller, Sholtz, Bunyan, Connors, Cook, Bussman, Graham, Pool. *Second row:* J. Capitani, Weatherington, O'Hair, Hamlin, Caven, Green, Sandstrom, Kennedy, N. Capitani, Gambogi, Wells, Hickey. *Front row:* Diemer, Ware, Kellar, Rocco, Pellegrini, Noriel, Camra, Looney, Cary, Lawson.

82   1 9 3 5

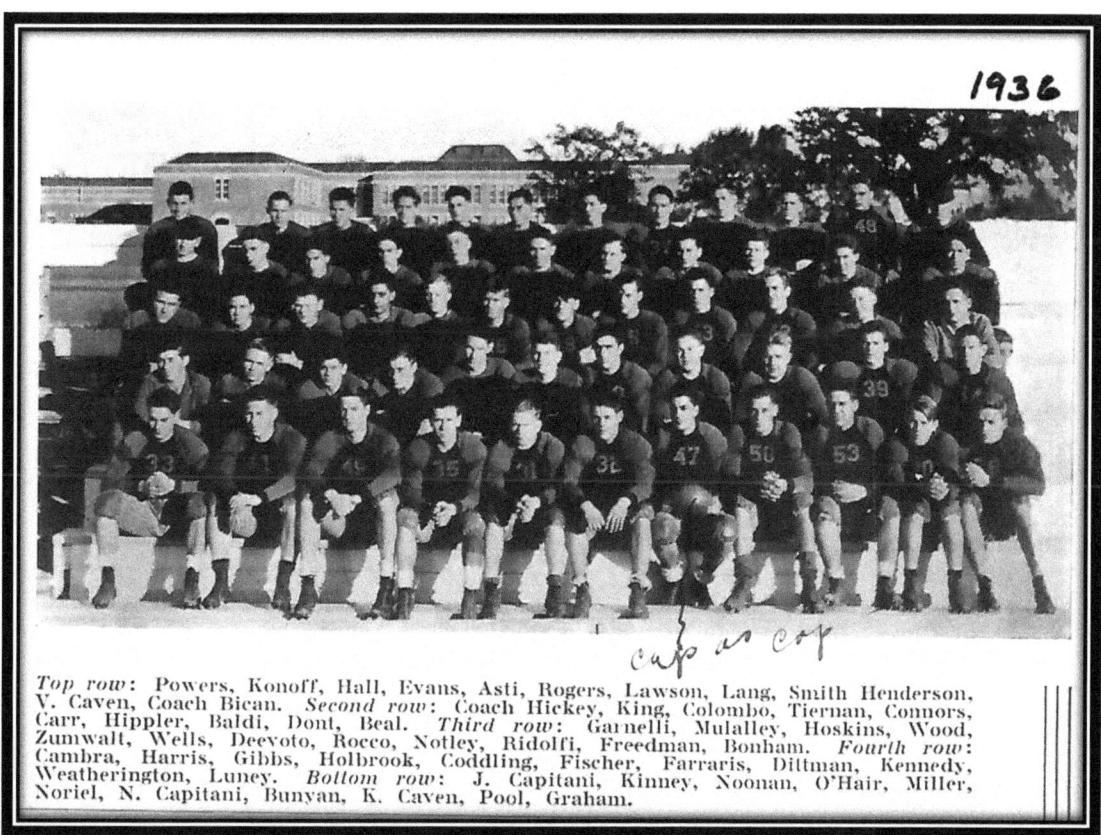

1936

Top row: Powers, Konoff, Hall, Evans, Asti, Rogers, Lawson, Lang, Smith Henderson, V. Caven, Coach Bican. *Second row:* Coach Hickey, King, Colombo, Tiernan, Connors, Carr, Hippler, Baldi, Dont, Beal. *Third row:* Garnelli, Mulalley, Hoskins, Wood, Zumwalt, Wells, Deevoto, Rocco, Notley, Ridolfi, Freedman, Bonham. *Fourth row:* Cambra, Harris, Gibbs, Holbrook, Coddling, Fischer, Farraris, Dittman, Kennedy, Weatherington, Luney. *Bottom row:* J. Capitani, Kinney, Noonan, O'Hair, Miller, Noriel, N. Capitani, Bunyan, K. Caven, Pool, Graham.

Window decal featuring Ernie Nevers Field

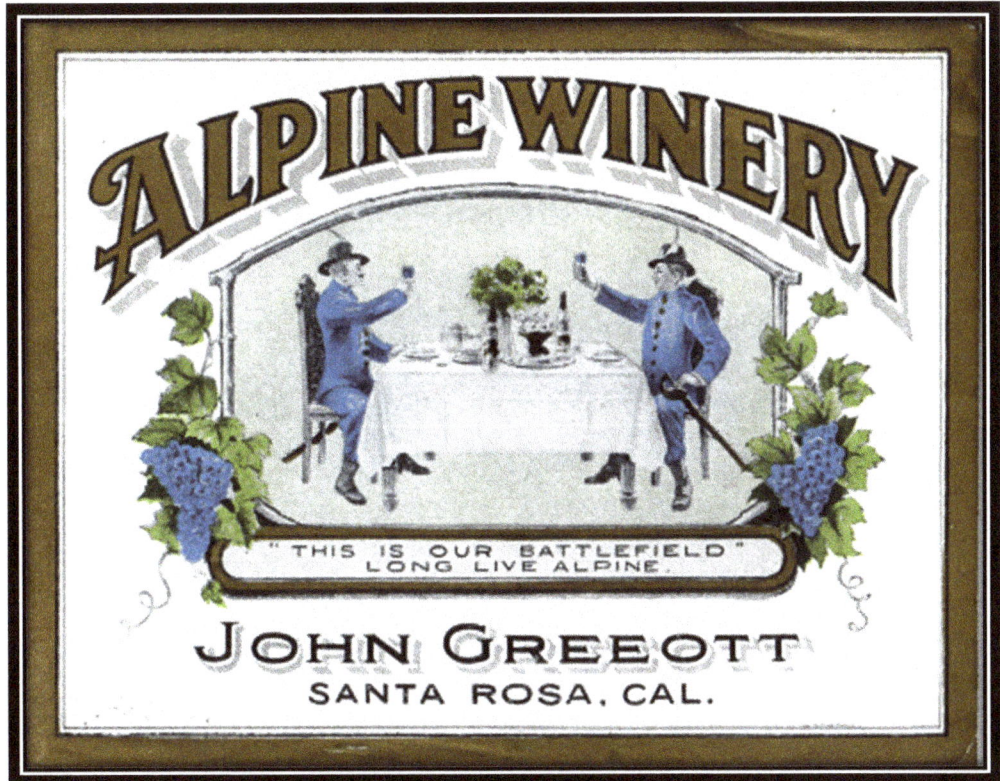

Located on North Street

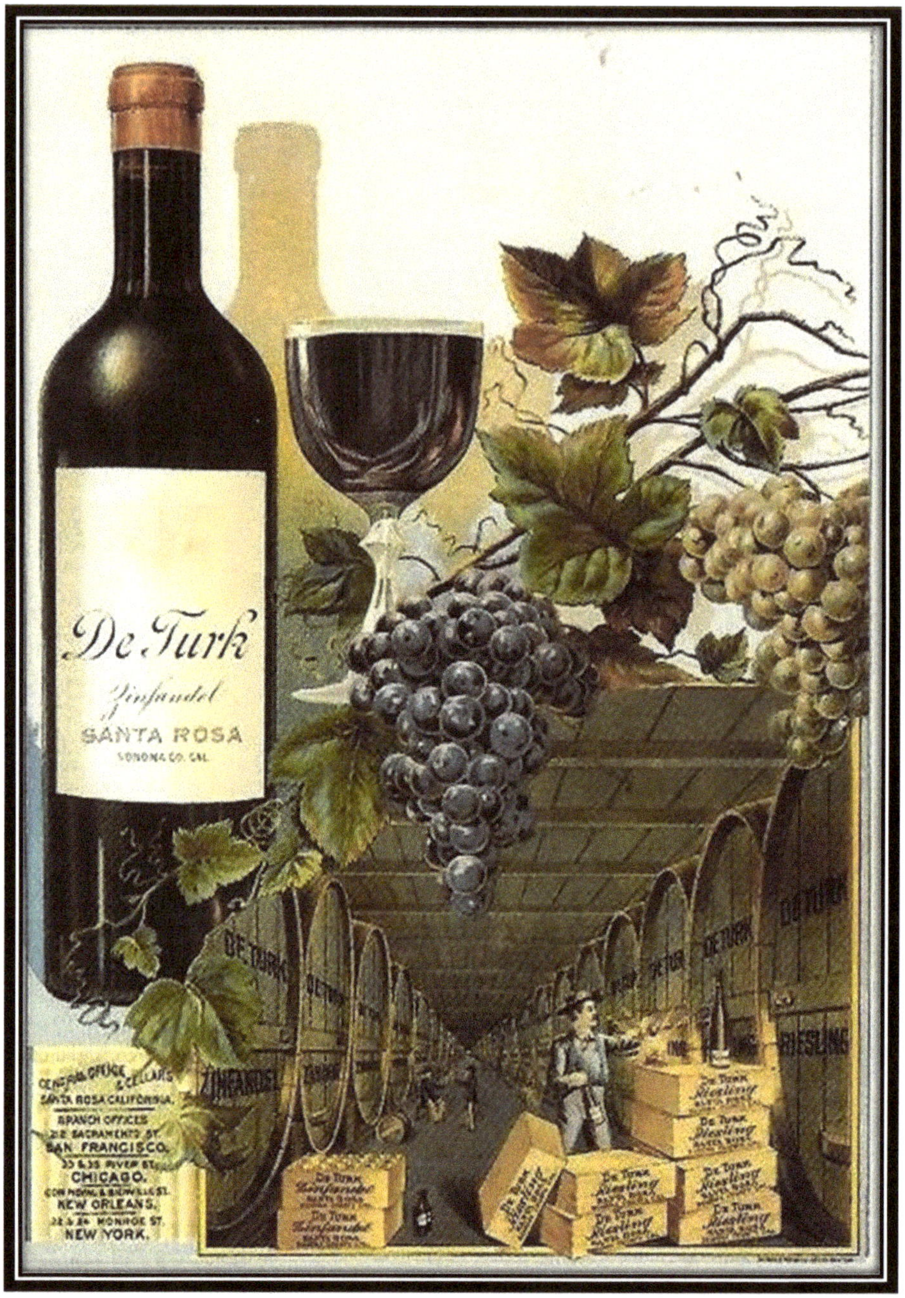
De Turk
Zinfandel
SANTA ROSA
SONOMA CO. CAL.
SANTA ROSA CALIFORNIA.
BRANCH OFFICES
SAN FRANCISCO.
CHICAGO.
NEW ORLEANS.
NEW YORK.
DE TURK
ZINFANDEL
RIESLING

ESTABLISHED 1876
DE TURK WINERY

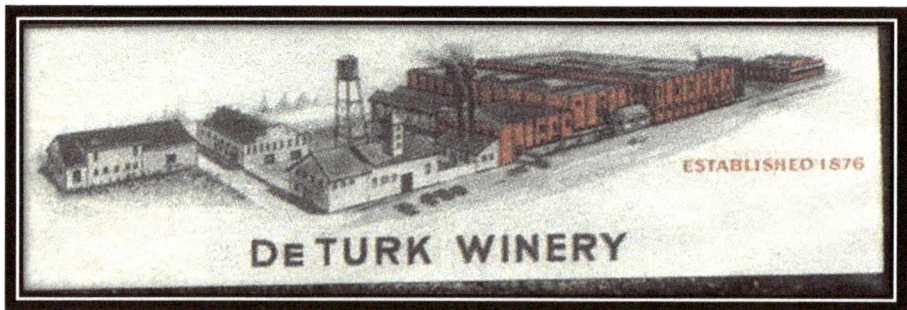

PERMIT NO.
CAL. U-1131

SONOMA VALLEY
BREWING CORPORATION
7 COLLEGE AVENUE
SANTA ROSA, CALIF.

STEAM BEER

Two unique brands of beer brewed in Santa Rosa and never distributed on a major market. Labels are one of a kind in Bob Welch collection.

NET CONTENTS 11 FL. OZS.

INTERNAL REVENUE
TAX PAID

PERMIT CALIF.
U-1112

BB
BEER
FOR HEALTH and HAPPINESS
BALDOCCHI BROTHERS
SANTA ROSA, CALIF.

GRACE BROS. BREWERY FOUNDING BROTHERS

Joseph T. Grace   **Frank P. Grace**

SONOMA COUNTY SHERIFF'S DEPARTMENT c.1905

Sheriff Frank Grace seated in center with deputies
S. Piezzi   W. L. Tombs   F. J. Cornwell   J. L. Gist
W. F. Wines   Frank P. Grace   Jeff Gage

1897 Line drawing of Grace Bros. Brewery & Icehouse

Rooftop Grace Bros. advertisement Fourth & Hinton Avenue

GRACE BROS. STOCK CERTIFICATES

JOSEPH T. GRACE SEPTEMBER 15, 1908

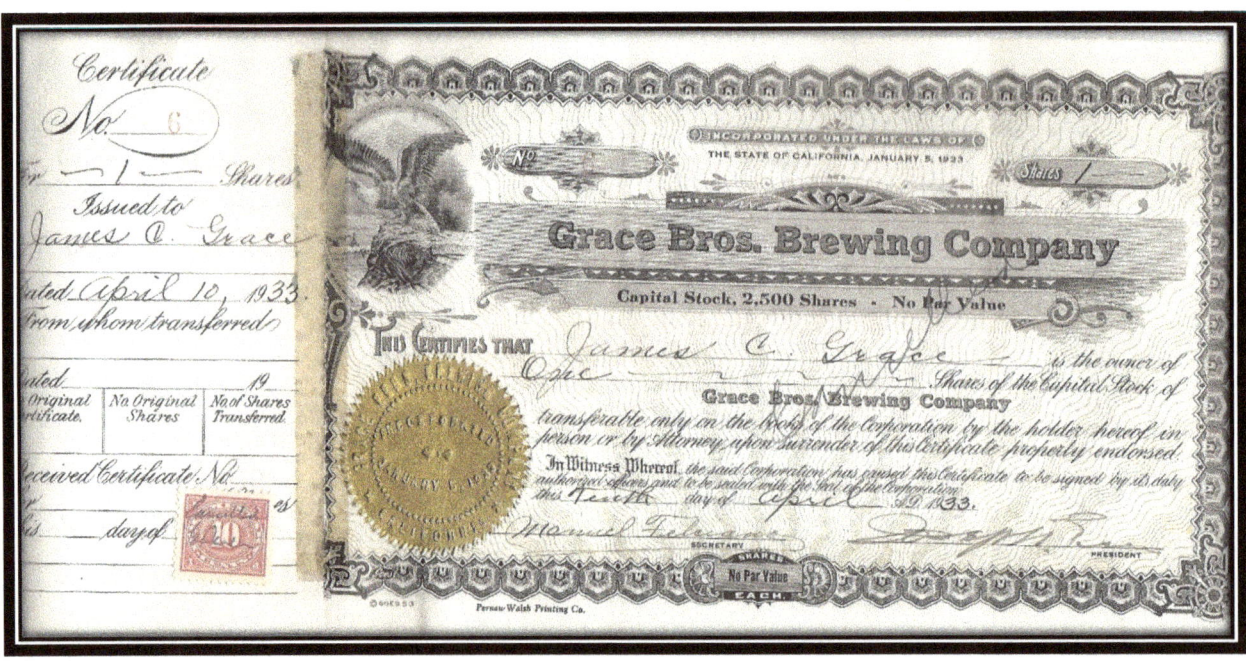

JAMES C. GRACE APRIL 10, 1933

GRACE BROS. BOTTLING LINE

BASIC REASONS WE HAVE PURE FOOD & DRUG LAWS

Pure Food & Drug laws were not in effect until 1906. When a bottle was returned it was placed in a saline solution overnight and then in the morning a boy, normally about 12 years old, would pick up the bottle, shake it, then drain it and place it face down on the wheel. Then a bottler nearest the wheel with the filling hoses would pick up a bottle and the hose at the same time and suck on the hose drawing the beer and filling the bottles. Most likely a very short shift.

HEADING FOR THE FIELD OF HOPS

Joseph T. Grace Residence 4th & College Avenue

Bud Shea – Jack Grace – Tom Grace – William Grace – Frank Grace

GRACE BROS. ADVERTISEMENT

Roadside Billboard Advertisement

GRACE BROS. AMBER QUART BOTTLES

A FEW OF GRACE BROS. BEER CANS

9th Annual
ENCAMPMENT
Northern Cal.
VETERANS
Association
GRACE BROS.' PARK
SANTA ROSA
JUNE 14-23
1905

LOCAL UNION No. 7
Brewers & Malsters
LOCAL UNION
No. 7
OF
CALIFORNIA

ROSE CITY SODA WORKS

HUTCH & GRAVITATING STOPPER BOTTLES

Top Row Hutch Bottles
Bottom Row Gravitating Stopper Bottles

WM. H. HUDSON SODA WORKS

Santa Rosa Soda Works, Hudson & Palmer, Proprietors.

PRIDE OF SANTA ROSA SODA BOTTLES
Santa Rosa Bottleing Company Serving Tray shown below

ELMER BROWN
ROSE CITY SODA WORKS

ROSE CITY

SODA

WORKS

BROWN & SON, PROPS.

SPECIAL ATTENTION
TO FAMILY TRADE

SODA WATER OF
ALL KINDS

D STREET   PHONE 13
Rear of Masonic Temple.

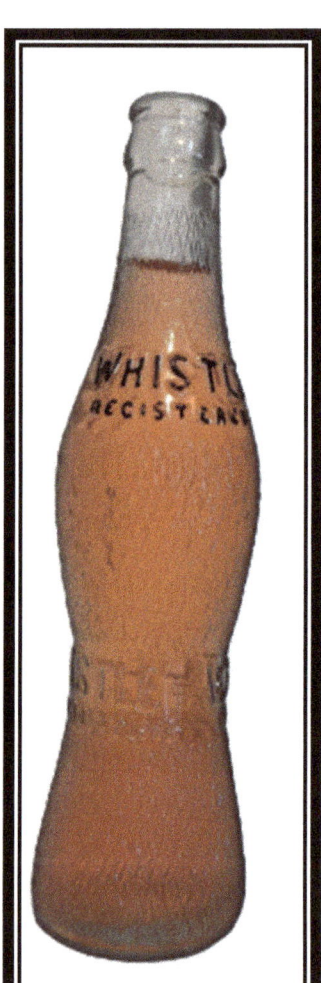

BROWN'S LIQUOR STORE

Brown's Liquor Store
Behind the counter - John Capitani – Norman Capitani
In front of counter - Unidentified – Chet Monahan

Brown's Liquor Store Give-Away Advertising Thermometers

GRACE BROS. SANTA ANITA ORANGE
GRACE BROS. LEMON SODA
GRACE BROS. LIME RICKEY
NEHI REDWOOD EMPIRE LIME RICKEY
JIMMY BRUCKER SONOMA CLUB GINGER ALE

SANTA ROSA SELTZER BOTTLES

 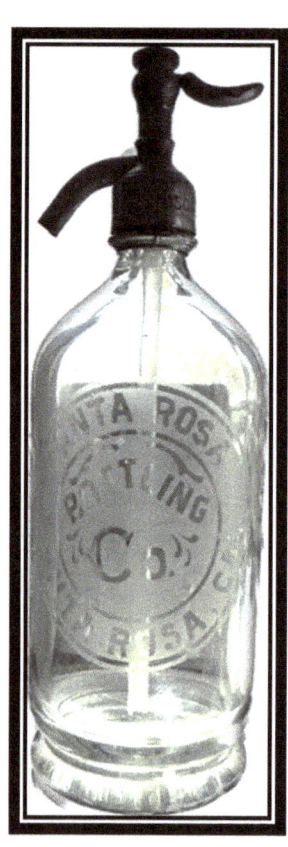 

SANTA ROSA SALOONS
GRAPE VINE SALOON
Mendocino Avenue

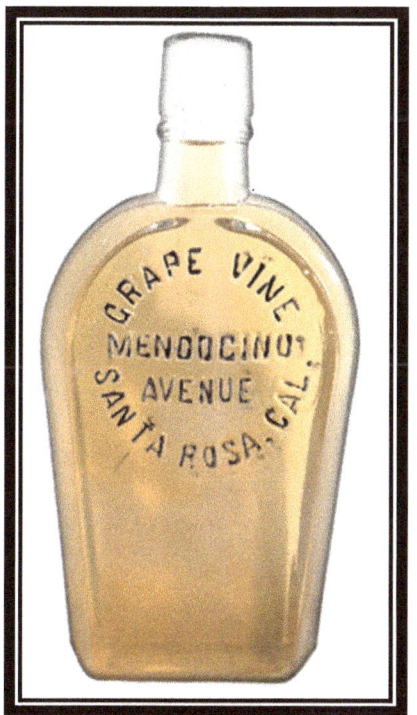

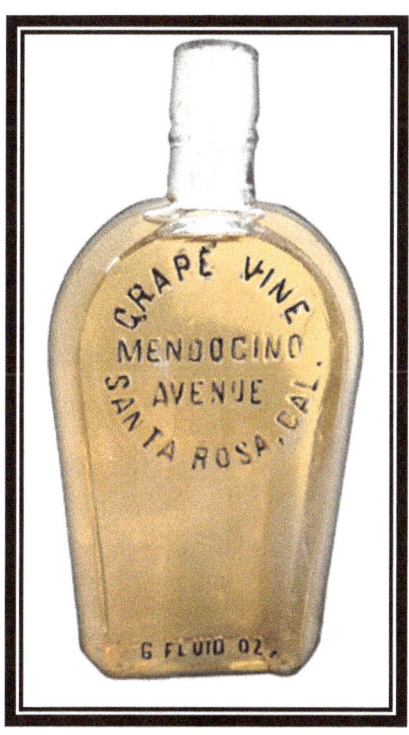

THE MODEL SALOON
523 Fourth Street

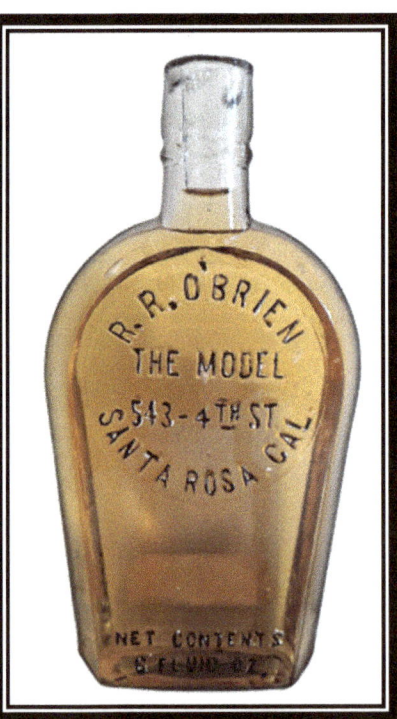

JAKE LUPPOLD'S

Senate Saloon next to Bowling Alley & Pool Hall First & Main Streets

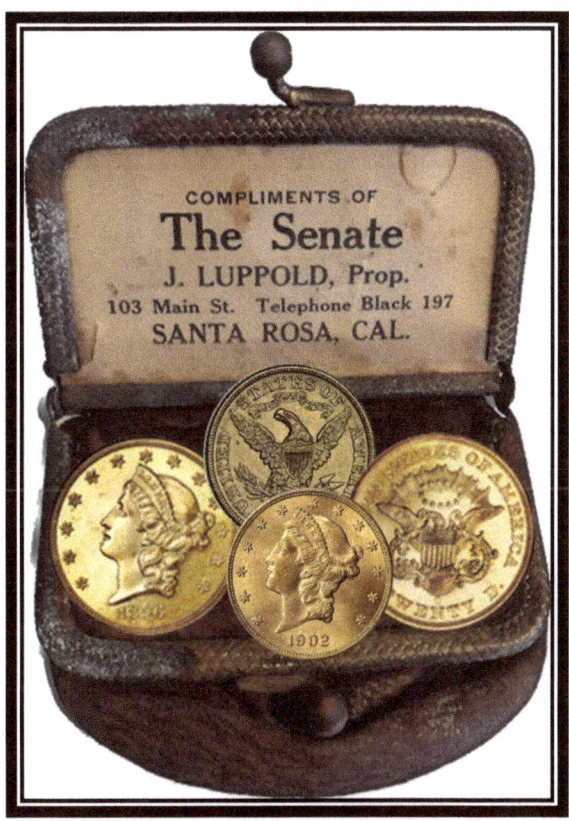

WESTERN HOTEL
Lower Fourth Street near Train Depot

NORTHWESTERN LIQUOR STORE GEMETTI'S
516 Third Street

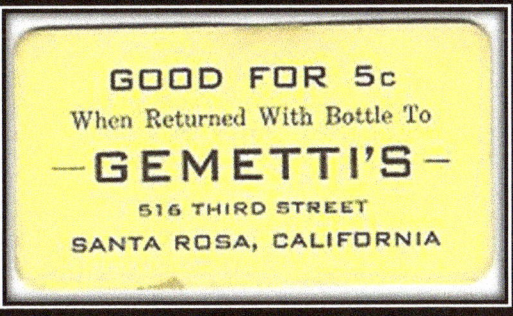

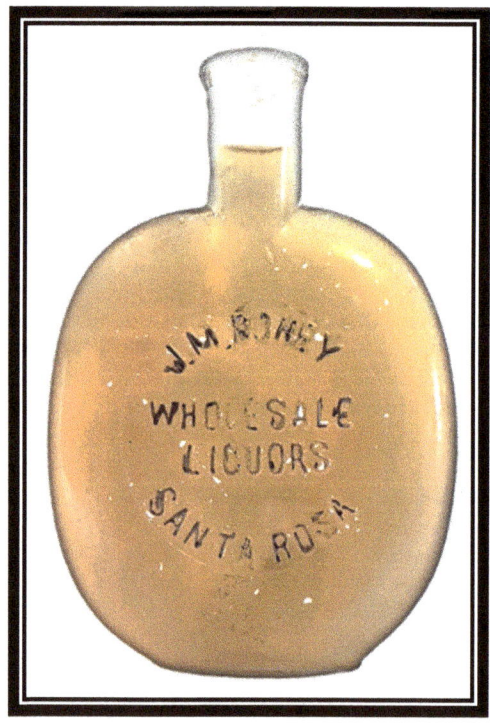

===

All tokens listed in this book are the collection of Merle Avila

MARK WEST SPRINGS
MRS. W. H. OTTERSON, Prop.
SANTA ROSA, CAL.

4

Largest Grape Vine Arbor in the World, at Mark West Springs

Beautiful MARK WEST SPRINGS

Nine Miles from Santa Rosa, California   MRS. W. H. OTTERSON, Prop.

"The Prettiest Place in California." Largest Wild Grape Arbor in the World. One of the big attractions is the fine large Mineral Water Swimming Tank, which has been installed, 30 by 60 feet.

Eight mineral springs; sulphur water tub bathes at temperature of 92 degrees; fine trout fishing and hunting; large pavilion, croquet grounds, etc.; mails daily and daily papers; telephone and telegraph; only three and a half hours from San Francisco, and but nine miles by auto from Santa Rosa. Auto meets trains from San Francisco at Santa Rosa by appointment. Stage passes our door.

The Springs are located on Mark West Creek, at an elevation of 800 feet above sea level. The redwood, oak, poplar, laurel and maple trees on the hills and along the banks of the flowing creek afford delightfully shaded walks and picnic grounds.

VIEW OF BATH HOUSE

The famous Patrified Forest, one of the world's wonders, is only five miles distant from the Springs. Visitors will be amazed at the extent and beauty of the California wild grape arbors, and they are really worth traveling a long way to see. There are seven of these arbors in all. The largest is formed by twelve mammoth vines, the trunks of which are entwined in graceful and regular coils around the pillars supporting the roof of the veranda. This is noted as being the largest wild grape vine arbor in the world, the dimensions being 50 feet in width and 170 feet in length. The hotel veranda (20 by 150 feet) and the broad driveway for the autos are entirely under the shade of this magnificent arbor. A dam, over which the water constantly flows, is placed in Mark West Creek at the hotel, and the boating and swimming is superb.

But the greatest of all the attractions are the wonderful Mineral Springs. There are eight in number. The largest of these has a flow of 5,000 gallons an hour, making it not only the largest mineral spring in Sonoma, but one of the largest in California. This spring supplies the large swimming tank. A feature is that the tank will always have continual fresh water, therefore assuring a most cleansing bath. The table and service will be, as usual, first-class in every particular.

MARK WEST CREEK SCENE

To reach the Springs take morning or afternoon Sausalito ferry (7:45 a. m. or 3:45 p. m.) for Santa Rosa, where auto meets trains by appointment. As there is a "Mark West" station on the railroad, to avoid confusion in buying tickets ask for "round trip to Mark West Springs." Fine auto road direct to springs; gasoline and oil supplied at a reasonable price.

Rates—$3.00 to $3.50 a day, or $15.00 to $17.00 per week; children under 7 years, half price; accommodations for 200 guests. There are hotel rooms, cottage rooms, and tent cottages. A pleasant outing assured all. Make reservations early. Personal attention given our guests.

Boating at Mark West Springs, Sonoma County, Cal.

Mark West Springs showing Grape covered Arbor and Stage, Sonoma County, Cal.

White Sulphur Springs Santa Rosa
(Kiwana Springs)

Inscribed on watch face
Geo. Hood & Sons
Santa Rosa, Cal.

Giveaways that held pocket watches with advertisement on the outside
of one's overalls, jeans or men's pants.

WATCH FOBS

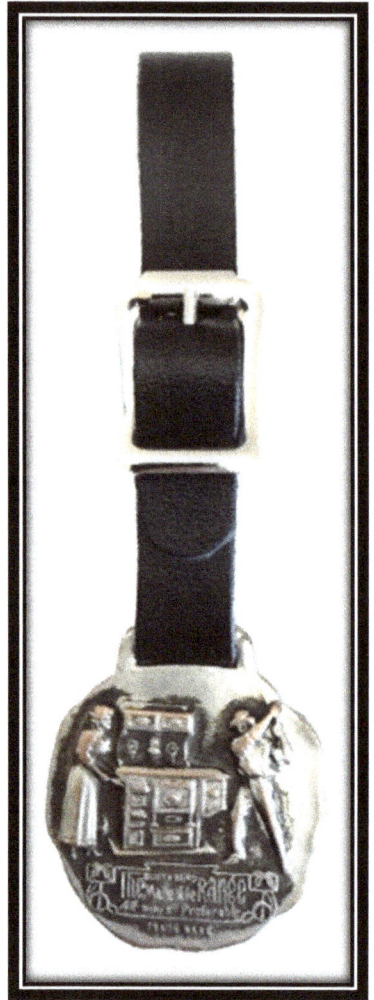

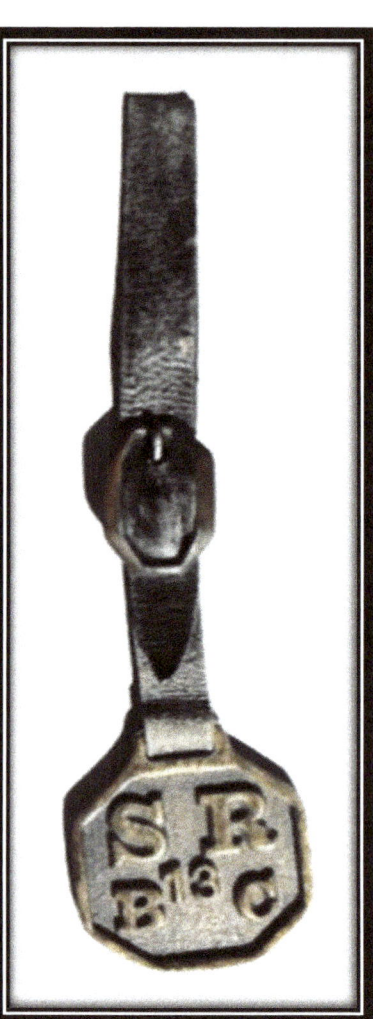

Ferrari & Perotta Bar

Dennis Kurland's Santa Rosa Bottling Company Serving Tray

**PRIVATE SANTA ROSA LABELS FOR BOTH
LENA'S AND TRAVERSO & ARRIGONI**

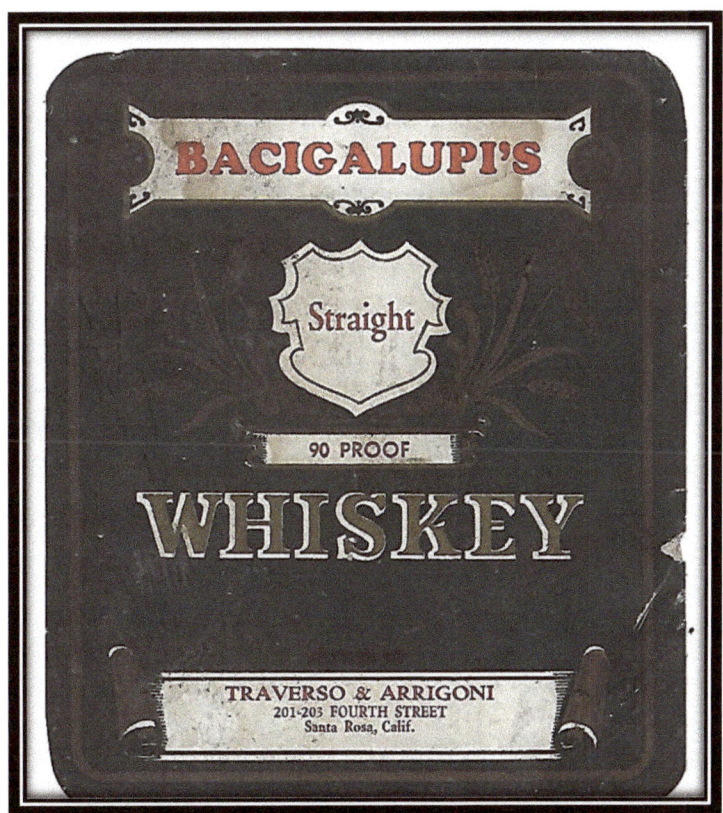

Additional Collectibles

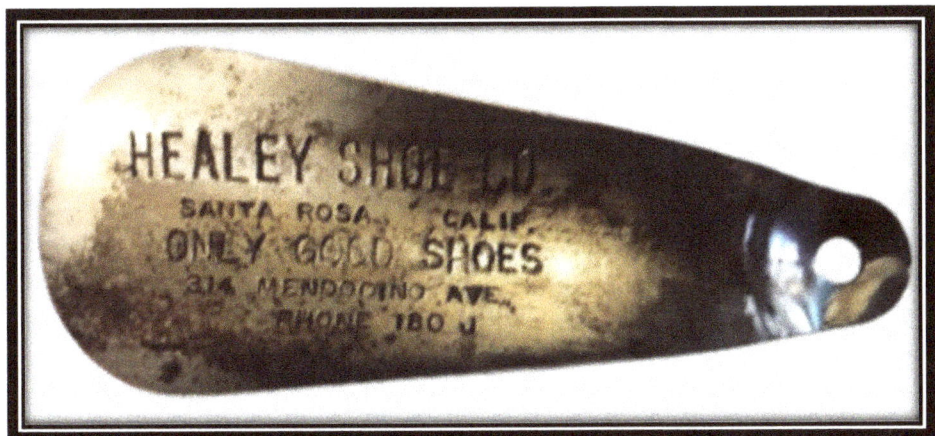

Healey Shoe Horn

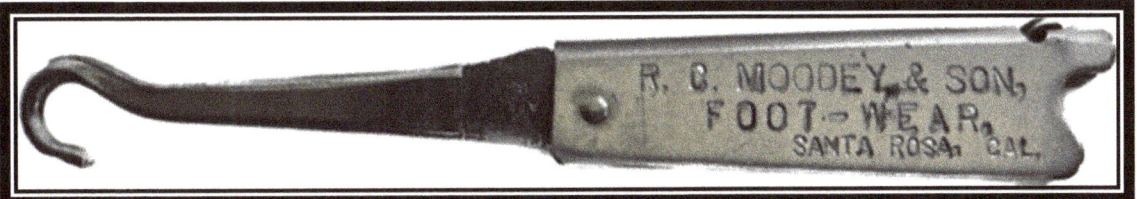

R. C. Mooney Button Hook

Needles & Bobbin Kit

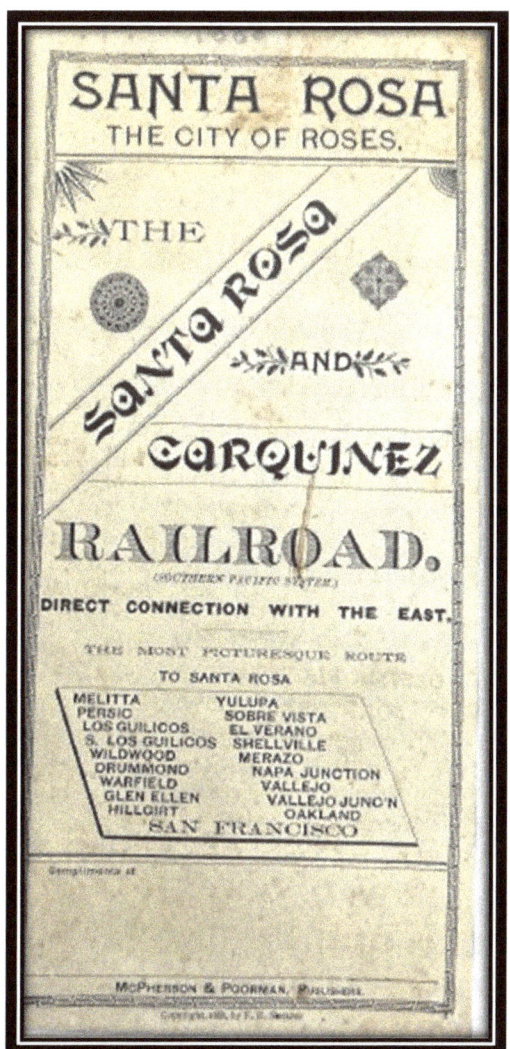

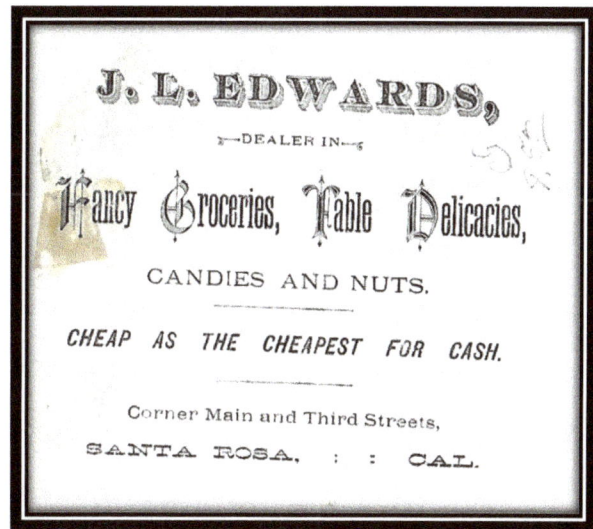

Santa Rosa High School Trophy c.1912

Prindle & Kurlander Trophy

Sonoma County Court House

Luther Burbank Home & Gardens

Luther Burbank Plate

Flagler's Santa Rosa

**Frank C. Loomis
531 4th Street**

Santa Rosa Old Adobe

Santa Rosa Flour Mills
Two blocks north of the railroad station

Mark McDonald, Sr. (1833 – 1917)

Mark McDonald Owner of Santa Rosa Water Works

Preserve this Receipt   No. _____ 2nd   Street

M. _____

TO SANTA ROSA WATER WORKS, DR.

FOR WATER RENT

From Jan. 1. 1916 to Feb. 1. 1916 . . . . $ 1.25

_____ Back Bills _____ $ _____

Feb. 3 _____ 1916 . . _____ $ _____

HOURS FOR IRRIGATION
7 to 9 a. m.; 4 to 7 p. m.   Paid _____

No.   In all cases Owners of property held for back bills